What On Earth
Is Happening?

What On Earth Is Happening?

Dr. Gale Newman

XULON PRESS

Xulon Press
2301 Lucien Way #415
Maitland, FL 32751
407.339.4217
www.xulonpress.com

Paperback ISBN-13: 978-1-6628-4075-3
eBook ISBN-13: 978-1-6628-4076-0

Table of Contents

Introduction

Many people in America are asking the question posed by this book's title, "What on earth is happening? Their question is directed, for example, at events they cannot understand like what is President Biden doing and why is he doing it? Because of the Executive Orders he has signed, many thousands of jobs have been lost to those working on the Keystone Pipe Line. Energy prices are going up and we are no longer energy independent. President Biden has lied to voters when, as a candidate for the office of President, he said he would work for the welfare of all Americans. Instead, as Mark Levin has documented in his book, <u>Marxist America</u>, President Biden has a different agenda other than the people of America. Therefore they ask the question, "What on earth is happening"? Also included in their questions is the subject of the criminal elements among our illegal immigrant population who are being releasing back into our society because of President Biden's executive orders. He is also relocating illegal immigrants throughout America without the consent of the governors whose states are being forced to care for them when deposited there. The same thing is now true of immigrants from Afghanistan. In the middle of a Pandemic where many Americans have been forced out of work, he is going to allow into our country tens of thousands of immigrants to compete for jobs. In addition to that his plan is to give illegal immigrants free health care and an education at the expense of the American tax payer. The grocery store cannot compel me to pay for another patron's grocery bill. So how can the President demand of me as an American citizen to pay for someone else's college education or medical bills? The price tag for all this is staggering. What he is planning will cost America's tax payers Trillions of dollars and could cause a massive recession. This recession is just starting to manifest itself evidenced in higher gas and food prices. Many are predicting an inflationary cycle comparable to that of the Jimmy Carter presidency. These are just the beginning of the unprecedented events that lie ahead for the people of America. Fox News analysts Sean Hannity, Tucker Carlson and Laura Ingram, to mention just a few, are diligent in describing what Biden's policies are doing to America. Many related events have led us to this point in history. Those events have resulted in our current social unrest. However, the Bible is very clear in its teaching that we reap what we sow (Galatians 6:7). We are reaping the results of having liars in our Congress because American voters put them there. Most of these people are not concerned about the people they are suppose to represent, but rather are concerned with lining their pockets with money from lobbyists. We are reaping judges unconcerned about truth and justice because American voters and presidents put them there to render verdicts favorable instead to the Democratic agenda. Questions about our election have surfaced because the elected officials who were to monitor those elections refrained from the duties of their office. The electorate put them there and we are reaping the consequences of their dereliction of duties. Though hundreds of affidavits were signed by those who witnessed voter fraud, their stories and voices were ignored by the authorities. Fox News showed its viewers countless visible evidences of illegal votes being counted, some being counted twice. They showed unfolded mail-in ballots laying flat on a table. Had they been mailed, there would have been a crease where they had been folded. According to the Cancel Culture, Americans are to put their heads in the sand like an Ostrich and forget what they saw.

We once were a Capitalistic country. Now we are on the road to Socialism. Who is responsible? The people who elected and appointed our new leaders are responsible. Therefore we as a nation are about to reap a whirlwind. Actions have consequences. The Bible teaches this fact from Genesis to Revelation. Allow me to give you are few examples of this fact from each of those books. In Genesis God told Adam and Eve there would be consequences for their actions. He instructed them with these words, "You are free to eat from any tree in the garden, but you must not eat from the tree of the knowledge of good and evil, for when you eat of it you shall surely die." (Genesis 2:16-17). The book of Romans teaches what those consequences were. When Adam and Eve sinned by eating from the fruit of the forbidden tree, the author of Romans, the Apostle Paul, wrote, "Nevertheless, death reigned from Adam to Moses, even over those who do not eat by breaking a commandment as did Adam, who was a pattern of the man to come. But the gift is not like the trespass. For the many died by the trespass of the one man, Adam." (Romans 5:14). "Just as sin entered the world through one man, and death through sin, and in this way death spread to all men, because all sinned." (Romans 5:8) These passages of Scripture from the Bible declare the truth that the actions of Adam recorded in Genesis had consequences. One consequence was death, the separation of man from fellowship with God. God was holy and man had become sinful. There was no possibility of uniting the two except through God's salvation plan. The Bible asks, "What does righteousness and wickedness have in common?" (2 Corinthians 6:14) Throughout the Bible, God teaches that there are consequences to our actions.

In Revelation 20, the Bible student finds another example of the fact that actions have consequences. The Great White Throne judgment depicted there is a future judgment based on the actions of those being judged. "And I saw the dead, great and small, standing before the throne and books were opened...The dead were judged according to what they had done as recorded in the books." (Revelation 20:12) Again the Bible makes the point that our actions have consequences. In the days ahead, America will be experiencing the consequences of its National Election and a subsequent election held in Georgia. Instead of a president that had demonstrated he knew what he was doing, evidenced by a flourishing economy, lower taxes, the lowest unemployment rates in recent history, a strong military, poignant trade embargos on China, Russia and North Korea, a border wall and a replacement of NAFTA, peace in the Middle East, etc., we are going to be led by a group of people with radical ideas about how to manage this country. There is no evidence that proves their ideas will work. Instead, there is ample evidence from history and Socialistic countries like Venezuela that demonstrate their ideas will fail to work. That fact seems to have eluded our leader's historical studies. Therefore, we are now left with leaders totally ignorant of how to manage this country, much less their own families. The recent bungling of our withdrawal from Afghanistan is but another illustration of the ineptitude among our nation's leadership.

But is that the bottom line? Is there more to this than meets the eye? The Bible again has insight for us as we contemplate the answer to that question. The Bible speaks of unseen forces that have been at work guiding the past history of this world. Currently, they are at work planting seeds of discord and unrest that will provide the fruit that will serve as the basis for future events. Through their deceptions they hope not only to influence America, but also every nation on our planet. Those "forces" are called angels. The angels mentioned in the Bible have two different allegiances. The angels who follow Satan are called demons. The angels that follow their creator, the Lord Jesus Christ are holy and work to enable God's plan for mankind to come to fruition. For example, in the

Book of Daniel, we are introduced to two angels who were working in opposition to God's plan. Those two angels mentioned in Daniel 10:20-21 are demons, fallen angels, ordered by Satan to indirectly guide the affairs of the nations of Greece and Persia. They were trained by Satan to influence the leadership of those nations by deceiving them to follow certain courses of action.

The narrative tracing the first deception by an evil angel called Satan occurs in Genesis Three. There Satan deceived Eve into eating the forbidden fruit from the Tree of Knowledge of Good and Evil. The deception occurred when she believed the lie told to her by Satan. Even after God had instructed Adam and Eve not to eat of the tree "or they would die," Satan persuaded them to eat by saying "they would not die, but become like God, knowing good and evil." (Genesis 3) Adam and Eve could have countered this deception by quoting exactly what God had said to them. Jesus in his High Priestly prayer recorded in John 17 stated that "God's word is true." The Bible demonstrates the Bible's trustworthiness as truth when we stand upon it and use it. If Adam and Eve had done what is recorded in James 4:7, which says, "Submit to God, resist the Devil, and he will flee from you," Satan would have fled from Adam and Eve. While tempting them, had they used God's word against the lies contained in his deception, Satan would have fled from them. That would have solved that problem. There is an old saying, "Since God said it, I believe it, and that is the end of it." That is the attitude we Christians must have to be victorious over the "fiery darts" the Devil hurls at us.

The fact of this kind of temptation where deception is used is recorded throughout the Bible. An example of Satan's deception which will occur just prior to the thousand year reign of Jesus Christ on earth, is recorded in the Book of Revelation. There the Bible teaches that Satan will deceive the nations and bring them against Israel to destroy the Jewish people. (Revelation 19) There the Bible prophecies Satan will be thrown into The Abyss, so that he cannot "deceive the nations any longer." (Revelation 20:3) This verse reveals many truths, one of which is the deceptive nature of Satan's activity throughout history. This is his nature. Jesus taught this in his words recorded in John 8:44. He said that Satan was a liar and a murderer. That is his nature and he will continue in activities that reflect his lying and deceitful nature. 1 Timothy 4:1 is a scripture that supports that statement with these words: "The Spirit clearly says that in later times some will abandon the faith and follow deceiving spirits and things taught by demons." The Book of Revelation adds that after the thousand year reign of Jesus Christ on the earth concludes, Jesus Christ will release Satan for awhile. What does Satan do once he is released? He returns to his former activity of deceiving the nations. Revelation 20:7 predicts this when it records, "When the thousand years are over, Satan will be released from his prison and will go out to deceive the nations in the four corners of the earth, Gog and Magog, to gather them for battle."

The manipulation of nations is accomplished as demons deceive the rulers of the world's nations to initiate courses of action which they have been deceived to think are appropriate. This statement makes clear what the objective of these demons is, and how they are active in accomplishing their work. Here in America their work is identical to that which they have been doing throughout history. Their work is an effort to lead the world away from their worship of God; and in our country away from the meaning found in the inscription on our coins, "In God We Trust." They work despite the origins of our country represented in the Mayflower Compact. Of the 102 shipmates on the Mayflower, 50 were men, 19 were women and 33 young adults and children. 41 of these people signed the Mayflower Compact. It began with these words, "In the name of God, Amen." Allow me to describe some of the other parts of the Mayflower Compact, "By the grace of God we have undertaken, for the glory of God and for the advancement of the Christian faith, to plant this first colony." America has forgotten its roots. It needs to be reminded of what God said to the people of Israel after they entered the land of Israel, "When you have eaten and are satisfied, praise the Lord your God for the good land he has given you. Be careful that you do not forget the Lord your God." (Deuteronomy 8:10-11) In the next few verses God elaborates that when they are settled down in nice houses and they are wealthy because of a great economic successes, they were not to forget the God who gave it to them. Here in America we need to do the same thing. For Satan tempts us to take great pride in what we have built here. Heed the warning to not forget God, who is Jehovah Jireh, which means God is our provider.

Around the world Satan's work is to create animosity between nations and people groups. The effectiveness of his work can be measured by the wars and skirmishes he has orchestrated. Less than 300 years of peace among nations have been recorded in the thousands of years of Earth's history. His work among members of the United Nations is observed in the many reprimands Israel constantly receives from this body even though it was this body that declared Israel a country in 1948. Nations of the world hate Israel because Israel believes it has a revealed religion substantiating its existence. Anything that even hints of the God of the Bible is openly resisted by those people who have been deceived by Satan, the open adversary of God. The remainder of this book is purposed to explain "what on earth is happening" as it relates to their work, its goal and the nature of Satan for whom they work.

Chapter One

At this point you might be asking, "Who is this being called the Devil or Satan and what is he trying to accomplish through his deceptions? I'll answer the first question now and the second later throughout this book. The Devil is an angel whom God created during the time he created the Heavens and the Earth. (Genesis 1:1) Angels are not mentioned in the Creation Accounts in Genesis One and Two. They are omitted because God did not want to distract us from the most important fact in those accounts. We know this because poetry exists in the narrative section of this Scripture. When that grammatical device occurs in a narrative portion, its purpose is to draw attention to what is written as being of great importance. That is what occurs in Genesis 1:27, "So God created man in his own image, in the image of God he created him; male and female he created them." The fact that this poetic statement is found in the midst of a narrative section was God's way of drawing attention to it. God was saying by so doing, "Don't miss this!" That means this statement is of utmost importance!

Many books and Theologians have written on the subject of the "Imago Dei", the Image of God. I will not regurgitate all that has been discussed about this subject, except to say God designed man in a special way. That design is called the "image of God." When Adam sinned, part of the Image of God designed into man was lost, and a certain part was retained. Genesis 9:6 reveals that part of the image which was retained with these words which are recorded there, "Whoever, sheds the blood of men, by men his blood shall be shed, for in the image of God has God made man." Part of what is the image of God is still retained in mankind, even after the Fall of Adam and Eve into sin in the Garden of Eden. That conclusion is based on the fact that even after the flood (Genesis 6) mankind still bears the image of God and this is the basis of judgment of someone who has killed another person. The meaning here is clear. When someone dies, a certain aspect of the Image of God reflected in the person who dies is removed from the earth. God desires his image be seen throughout the world. That is why he instructed man to multiply and fill the earth. (Genesis 1:28) And that is why the Image of God cannot be removed from the earth except under this condition mentioned in Genesis 9:6, "Whoever sheds the blood of man, by man shall his blood be shed, for in the image of God has God made man."

That part of the Image of God man retained after he sinned was his cognitive ability called rationality, his sense of morality and his sense of immortality. What was lost of the Image of God when Adam sinned in what is called "The Fall", was his relationship with God; he also lost his creaturely Holiness as well as competence. What Salvation restores is that part of the Image of God lost when Adam sinned, bearing witness to the fact that God still wants his Image to fill the earth. That restoration occurs as each member of the Godhead works to restore that which was lost in the person who has placed faith in Jesus Christ.

God the Father is the main person in the Godhead with whom a Christian experiences relationship. When Jesus taught his disciple to pray he instructed them to start with these words, "Our Father." (Matthew 6:9-13) In other words when we pray to God we are to address him as "Father." The Bible teaches that when a person becomes a Christian, they are "born again" and become a part of

God's family. (John 3:3) When Jesus was teaching about what God is like, on many occasions he spoke to his audience using parables. One of the parables he taught is recorded in Luke 15. That parable is about a Prodigal son. In that parable God is depicted as a father waiting for his son to return back home. When the son does return, the father is said to "run" towards his son. The act of an adult running was something unacceptable for a man to do in that culture. This part of the story is descriptive of what God did for mankind by dying on the cross for their sins. That God would humble himself to die in this way was extremely difficult for the Jewish people of this culture to accept, much like a man running. The fact that Jesus speaks of a Father "running" is to embrace the thought God was going to do something incredible which the people of that time would have great difficulty accepting. Specifically, that God would become a humble man and die for the sins of mankind on a cross. This was hard for them to believe. Instead they wanted a Messiah to demonstrate the powers of God and completely destroy the power and presence of Rome in their land. The Parable continued when Jesus described the Father throwing his arms around his son and kissing him. In the original Greek text, the tense of the verb teaches he continued to kiss the prodigal. What a beautiful visual of what a loving father our God is. Sit in his lap as a child and feel him affectionately kiss and hug you! Now remember that as the Father embraces the son, his beautiful and clean garment became soiled from the dirt, grime and odors emanating from the body and clothes of his son. What a picture of what Jesus did on the cross. The Bible declares God laid on him the sins of mankind. Isaiah 53:4-6 declared this truth with these recorded words: "He was despised and rejected by men; a man of sorrows and familiar with suffering. Like one from whom men hide their faces he was despised, and we esteemed him not. Surely he took up our infirmities and carried our sorrows, yet we considered him stricken by God, smitten by him and afflicted. But he was pierced for our transgressions; he was crushed for our iniquities. The punishment that brought us peace was upon him, and by his wounds we are healed. We all like sheep have gone astray, each of us has turned to his own way; and the Lord has laid on him the iniquity of us all." The Apostle Peter wrote that "Christ died for sins once and for all, the righteous for the unrighteous, to bring us to God."(1 Peter 3:18). Jesus Christ's mission was to restore your relationship to God as Father. Romans 8:15 declares "For you did not receive a spirit that makes you a slave again to fear, but you received the Spirit of Sonship. And by him we cry 'Abba Father'."

God the Son is another member of the Godhead who restores another dimension of the Image of God lost in the Fall. He restores our significance by giving us his holiness. He accomplished this by his death on the cross. Because of his atoning death Jesus can now forgive us our sins. To be without sin is to be holy. Once we are holy, the Bible instructs the Christian to present himself in that condition as he worships God. "Therefore, I urge you brothers, in view of God's mercy, to present yourselves as living sacrifices, holy and pleasing to the Lord as your spiritual act of worship." (Romans 12:1) The Apostle Paul wrote to the church at Ephesus, "You were taught with regard to your former way of life, to put off your old self, which is being corrupted by its deceitful desires, to be made new in the attitude of your minds; and to put on the new self, created to be like God in true righteousness and holiness." (Ephesians 4:22-24) The work of the Son occurs in our inner being where the Christian comes to know the love "that surpasses knowledge—that you may be filled with all the fullness of God." (Ephesians 3:15) A few verses later, the Apostle Paul informs us that the work of the church is to present each believer as a member of the body of Christ as having "the whole measure of the fullness of Christ." (Ephesians 4:13) Holiness is the only thing of value in the entire world. God begins this letter to the church at Ephesus declaring his desire to share that attribute with every believer in the church. He wrote that

4

the blessing of God was discovered in his work of "having chosen us before the foundations of the world that we should be holy and blameless." (Ephesians 1:4) What was lost in "The Fall", namely our creaturely holiness, God restores through the work of our Lord Jesus Christ. To fulfill God's will relative to holiness in the life of the believer is to be the mission and work of the church.

The Holy Spirit is that member of the Godhead who addresses our need to be competent. This was lost in the Fall. The Holy Spirit makes us competent by giving us "Spiritual Gifts" and the power to use them effectively in the Church. Our competency as Christians depends on using the Spiritual Gifts the Holy Spirit assigns to us. (1 Corinthians 12-14) The pastors in the church are assigned the task of helping the Christians in the church to identify their gifts and then use their gifts effectively. (Ephesians 4:11-12). Then God gives us the power needed to implement those gifts. (Ephesians 3:20-21) The Apostle Peter exhorts us to use our gift when he wrote his first epistle, "As each one has received a spiritual gift, employ it in serving one another, as good stewards of the manifold grace of God." (1 Peter 4:10)

Only God can meet those needs and restore what was lost in "The Fall". Therefore the First of Ten Commandments instructs people to go to no other place to have those needs met. Exodus 20:1 reads "I am the Lord your God, who brought you out of Egypt, out of the land of slavery. You shall have no other gods before me." The Psalmist learned why one should have no other gods when he wrote, "Trust in the Lord and do good; dwell in the land and enjoy safe pasture. Delight yourself in the Lord and he will give you the desires of your heart." (Psalm 37:3-4) Only God can meet the deep longings of our heart. Those longings are for relationship, significance and competence. To go to anything or anyone else is idolatry. The Apostle Paul warns the believers in Philippi of this. (Philippians 3:17-19) To him there were but two issues to face during our lifetime. One was Salvation and the other "destruction".

For him, the most dreadful of all thoughts was to remain in that latter condition throughout one's life. It brought him to tears to think that some people would take "the broad road that leads to destruction" that Jesus taught about in Matthew 7:13.

Satan had no idea what the Image of God was or how God alone could satisfy the needs in mankind which existed by virtue of being created by God in his image. Satan had no comprehension of what it meant to be created in the Image of God or how to meet the longings associated with it found in the human heart. It made sense that if God had designed us and made us for himself (Colossians 1:16), that only He alone would be able to meet our needs according to that design. Therefore, when Satan came to God and asked him for permission to be the god of this world, he had no clue about what that entailed. We know that Satan did this and that a conversation occurred between him and God about this role Satan wanted to play among God's created order. Based on the Scriptures and our ability to use deductive reasoning, we can deduce this fact. Since he was a created being, Satan was a finite being. As such he had limited abilities. One inability he has is the inability to be in more than one place at one time. Therefore as the late comedian Flip Wilson used to say, "The devil made me do it" is a lie. That saying is a deception. For him to believe the devil was personally tempting him to sin, as he does everyone else, was to illogically deviate from what the Bible declared about the Devil. He cannot be everywhere tempting people to sin.

The prophet Ezekiel declared Satan to have been created when he penned these words God had spoken to him, "You were the model of perfection, full of wisdom and perfect in beauty. You were in Eden, the garden of God; every precious stone adorned you... your settings and mountings were made of gold; on the day you were created they were prepared. You were anointed as a guardian cherub, for so I ordained you. You were on the holy mount of God; you walked among the fiery stones. You were blameless in your ways from the day you were created till wickedness was found in you." (Ezekiel 28:15) The specific wickedness found in Satan is given to us in Isaiah 14:13-14. There the Prophet Isaiah wrote this about the Devil, "You said in your heart, 'I will ascend to heaven; I will raise my throne above the stars of God; I will sit enthroned on the mount of the assembly, on the utmost heights of the sacred mountain. I will ascend above the tops of the clouds; I will make myself like the Most High." The sin of Satan was his pride. Therefore he said of himself that he was "like" God. To use a psychological term, his "idealized self" estimated the being he was to be equal to that of his creator. The reference to "stars" in this passage is a reference to all the angelic host God created. Like Mohammed Ali in boxing circles claimed he was "the greatest", so the Devil, relative to all God created, said he was the "greatest". What a contrast to what will be said of him at the judgment found recorded for us in Isaiah 14:15-17 "But you are brought down to the grave, to the depths of the pit. Those who see you stare at you, they ponder your fate; 'Is this the man who shook the earth and made the kingdoms tremble, the man who made the world a desert, who overthrew its cities and would not let the captives go home?" The prophet Isaiah is describing in these verses the advent of Satan into Hell where he will be spending a lot of time. Those that are already there are responding to his presence now among them. It was his deception and the lie he told them, namely that they didn't need to depend on God's word for Salvation that put them in Hell.

Questions:

1. Explain Satan's beauty marks that contributed to his belief that he was equal to God.

   _____

   _____

2. What has God done to fill the earth with the full Image of God?

   _____

   _____

   _____

3. In Matthew 7:13, to what does the word "destruction" refer?

   _____

   _____

4. The characterization of God as Father in Luke 15 is described behaviorally. How is it described?

   _____

   _____

   _____

5. Is it meaningful for you to think of God as your Father? Why?

   _____

   _____

   _____

6. Ephesians 1:4 declares God's purpose for you! What is his plan to accomplish this?

   _____

   _____

   _____

7. What are the implications of Satan being a created entity?

_____

_____

_____

Chapter Two

B etween the end of Chapter Two of Genesis and the beginning of Chapter Three, a dialogue between God and Satan occurred. The Bible alludes to this and asks us to put on our thinking caps and use deductive reasoning to conclude what was said between them. For example, Genesis One and Two give a blueprint of the creation of the heavens and earth by God. After describing all that that entailed, God reviewed his work and declared all that he had created was "good". However, without explanation, in Chapter Three of Genesis, one is introduced to a being that is not "good". The careful Bible student discerns this fact by listening in on the conversation that ensued between the Serpent (Satan) and Eve. That serpent is identified later in the Bible as the Devil. Revelation 20:1-2 reveals an angel that "seized the dragon, that ancient serpent, who is the devil, or Satan, and bound him for a thousand years". Therefore, we know this serpent in Genesis 3:1, to be in fact the devil, based on the evidence provided in the Bible. How this entity called Satan was able to get permission from a Sovereign God to be in the Garden of Eden is not revealed. The fact that Satan is there must be based on the fact that God permitted him to be there. What was the conversation between God and Satan that resulted in God allowing Satan to be in the Garden of Eden? This Garden was created by God to be the home for Adam and Eve. The environment of the Garden provided for their needs. There were plants and fruit trees and rivers that were designed by God to be used for food and water. God had made the garden a safe place for them to dwell. The curse on nature had not yet been pronounced since Adam and Eve had not yet sinned. Therefore there was benevolence and peace among the animals and between them and Adam and Eve. The Garden of Eden was a safe haven for them to live. Consequently, they did not know the feeling of fear or anxiety. God had provided all they needed and walked with them daily in the Garden to explain the health benefits that they would receive by eating the different foods. He further explained the traits of each of the animals and how to live in peace with them.

However, God had warned them about one tree in the Garden of Eden from which they were not to eat. They were instructed not to eat of the tree of the knowledge of good and evil, warning them that "they would surely die if they did eat from it". (Genesis 2:17) Those words gave them the directions they needed to live at peace with God and Nature. Since words have meaning, when God encoded this instructional message he wanted to send to Adam, we know he chose words that explained exactly the meaning of what he had said and what would happen if his words went unheeded. God had created Adam and Eve with the ability to understand the language they could use to communicate with each other and God. So when God used the word translated "die", we can reason Adam knew exactly what God was saying to him. An illustration of this comes from the Ten Commandments. When God used the word translated "Thou shall not kill" in the sixth commandment. There were 10 other words in the Hebrew language that could be translated into the word "kill", but he chose the one that meant "First Degree Murder". In other words, no man has the right to plan and then to act out the taking of the life of another person. If he does, God wrote further, "I will demand an accounting for the life before his fellow man". Then God added, "Whoever sheds the blood of man, by man his blood shall be shed; for in the Image of God has God made man". (Genesis 9:6) What this means is amplified later as God gave his law through Moses to the nation of Israel. God said that only a group of judges could decide guilt worthy of death by the witness of at least two witnesses. When guilt was established in this way, then men corporately could and should take that man's life.

Returning now to the Genesis Three account, this question still looms: How did Satan obtain God's permission to be in the Garden of Eden to tempt Adam and Eve to sin? This garden was home to the first family on earth. God had provided everything they needed to live their lives. Though they had food and water, there was no need for clothing since they had not experienced the feeling of shame and guilt for any sin they would have committed. In the Garden of Eden was found an environment where no emotion of fear could be found because God had also provided his Word for their safety. His word would provide direction for them if there was any doubt what God's will was. If Eve ever went to God and asked what his will was for feeding dinner to Adam, God would repeat what he said to Adam. "From any tree in the garden...", you may eat. If she pressed the issue by asking if she should give him a nice fruit salad, God would always answer the same, "From any tree in the garden you may eat, except..." God's will was always clear from what he said. This same verse was their safety net against the temptation posed by Satan as well. Quoting this verse to Satan at this time in Genesis Three or any time would have been enough to stop the temptation. Quoting Scripture was the same thing Jesus did when he was tempted to sin by Satan. Matthew 4:1-11 records the words Jesus used to thwart Satan's attempts to entice him to sin. After fasting 40 days, Jesus was hungry. Satan tempted Jesus to depend on himself to get bread as opposed to waiting on God to meet his needs. Jesus said God would provide and he would wait on him. Satan then took Jesus to the temple and at the highest point of the temple, told Jesus to throw himself off the temple because God promised to take care of him. Jesus said that promise was good and he didn't have to test God to prove it. Satan further tempted Jesus to evade the cross and the future pain and suffering he would experience at the hands of the Pharisees and Romans. Satan knew Jesus knew what the prophet Isaiah had written concerning his future treatment, suffering and death on a cross. Satan was therefore offering Jesus a way to avoid that humiliation, suffering and death. Jesus was tempted to do this by bowing down to Satan and worshipping him. Jesus silenced Satan's attacks by again quoting the Bible where we are instructed to worship God alone.

Psalm 119:11 states "thy word have I hidden in my heart, that I might not sin against thee." The "word" to which the Psalmist is referring is the Word of God contained in the Bible. When you know what God has said, then the Bible becomes a "lamp to your feet, and a light for your path". (Psalm 119:105) God had given his word to Adam and Eve. It would have kept them safe from Satan's temptation had they used it and followed it. But they failed to do so. The consequences of their action resulted in Jesus Christ, God's Son, having to come to this earth and give his life a ransom for all who had sinned. He had to die to pay the penalty for their sin as well as for our sin. Because Jesus did so, everyone can place faith in that work and be saved from the penalty of their sin. That is why he came to earth and he succeeded in his mission, much to the dismay of Satan. The reason for his dismay is because of Christ's work on the cross. Jesus Christ's work on the cross totally "disarmed Satan and his fallen angels". (Colossians 2:15) Anyone trusting in Jesus' work will be "rescued from being under the authority of the kingdom of this world, ruled by Satan, and then placed into the kingdom of God whose king is Jesus Christ. This redemption resulted in the forgiveness of our sins. (Colossians 1:13-14)

Again, how did Satan obtain permission from a Sovereign God to enter the Garden of Eden and tempt Eve to sin? We must deduce a conversation between God and Satan had occurred giving him permission to be there and to conduct this interview with Eve. If I showed up at a baseball field dressed in the uniform of one of the teams, members of that team would automatically have to believe I have permission from the coach to be there. How else would I have the uniform and know the place and time of the game to be played. They would know a conversation between me and coach had occurred. In the same way we can reason that a conversation between God and Satan had occurred giving him permission to be there in the Garden of Eden. This was not the Devil's garden. God had designed it to be the home for Adam and Eve. It was God's garden.

The conversation between God and Satan must have sounded something like this:

Satan: "Thank you your Most High God for agreeing to give me an audience".

God: "You are most welcome, Lucifer, O Morning Star. However, the answer is NO"!

(Morning Star was the name given to Satan by God. Isaiah 14:12)

Satan: "You don't know my question. Don't you think your answer is premature? Allow me the time to pose my question!

God: "Your question reflects your limitations as a created angel. As God, I am omniscient. I know everything. I am able to know everything you think before you think it. Understanding this is beyond your capability. Even by me naming this attribute of mine to you, you have no ability to process all that this means. That is how I was able to know your precise question before you asked it."

(Psalm 139:4, "Before a word is on my tongue, you know it completely, O Lord")

Satan: "Since you think you know everything, tell me what my purpose is in being here"?

God: "Trying to test me, Lucifer? Your words evidence pride in you. Your challenge evidences you do not believe my words to be true. When I created you and the other angels, I taught every one of you that everything I said was true. They could count on it. The fact that you are questioning my trustworthiness evidences you think yourself to be my judge, my superior."

("Every good and perfect gift is from above, coming down from the Father of heavenly Lights, who does not change like shifting shadows.") James 1:17

Satan: "That is correct and that is why I came to you with my question. So what is it"?

God: "Your question of me was based on my Sovereignty as God. You wanted my permission to reign as god over the inhabitants of the earth. And my answer was "no" a few minutes ago, and it still remains no."

Satan: "You do not know all that was involved in my question."

God: Yes I do. Remember I know your thoughts even before you think them. You wanted to reign as god in my place, telling the people of earth that even though I had created them, I had appointed

16

you to rule the earth in my stead, and that all worship of you as god would be deflected to me."

Satan: "That is correct. You are busy. This would be a creative way, pardon the pun, for you to focus on other things like the vast number of stars in the second heaven. In fact, I noticed recently one of the stars showing signs that it will explode soon."

God: "A number of stars will be exploding soon. One of the largest stars, R136al, located in the Megellic Cloud, which is 315 times larger than the earth's sun, will create quite a spectacle when it blows up. It will be a super-novae. However, the earth is safe since it is 163,000 light years away."

Satan: "That is what I mean. Your attention is needed elsewhere. Putting me in charge for awhile would help you."

God: "I do not need any help from you or any created being. Don't you remember what I said to you on the day I created you and the other angels? Every atom and every particle constituting an atom is controlled by me. Even UY Scuti which is 1700 times larger than earth's sun, and VY Canis Majoris, with heat at 3500 Kelvin, I control. Eta Carina, which is 2500 light years away and shines one million times brighter than earth's sun, though it is only 250 times the size of a G2V star, is controlled by me. Earth's sun is called a yellow dwarf. It pales in comparison to the stars I just mentioned. It is called a G2V star and I watch over it as well. Even the material with which you were created was designed by me and is under my control. The problem with you, Satan, is that you have a dwarfed understanding of who I am. The fact of my omni-science, my omnipotence and my omnipresence has not impacted your thinking about me. Many in the future will reflect your small

"God" mentality to their detriment. It is that thinking coupled with many other thoughts that lead me to say "no" to your request."

Satan: "What other thoughts to which are you referring?"

God: "During the six days I created everything, I created you and the angelic host. My abilities to design and form everything that lives on land and in the sea never did impress you. Everyone who meditates on the magnitude of that accomplishment should be in awe of me, but not you and those angels who have chosen to follow you in your rebellion against me. You have convinced them that because angels are stronger and smarter than mankind, even though mankind carries with them the Image of God, they should not have to "minister" to men and women, but instead they should worship you."

Satan: "Again you are correct."

God: "I am always correct. Get used to it."

Satan: "You think that you're so great. You think your plan for all that you created is so great and it will have a tremendous ending and will be gratifying to all. I too have a plan. I will humble you and exist as a co-equal god with you. You need to get used to that!"

God: "I know all about your plan. Your "small god" mentality will ultimately bring you to ruin. You could not possibly be a successful god to the people of this world. Every person that will ever live on this earth will bear the Image of God. That image will manifest its presence in them in desires only I can meet. Those needs are for a deep relationship based on my attribute of love, for value and esteem based on my attribute of holiness and for a sense of competence, based on my attribute of power. A part of that image will be reflected in their rational abilities, a sense of morality and a sense of immortality. These last three abilities do not depend upon me to be experienced and manifested in mankind as do the other three. To experience these last three abilities is to manifest the image of God which they have because of my creation."

Satan: "This is where you have made an error in judgment. I am able to meet the needs you identified in people and probably even better than you."

God: "That is your pride talking, Lucifer. You forget I designed you when I created you. Indeed, because of your beauty, power and mental abilities, I assigned you to be the guardian of my throne. However, as a created being, your relational abilities are limited. Your abilities are the same as I designed into mankind. They are able to experience approximately twelve close relationships at one time. Like mankind, you have the same limitations. So how are you going to meet all the needs of people populating the world when that number reaches millions? And how are you going to love with my kind of love? My love is not like Eros or Friendship love. It is a special kind of love based on my nature. It is called Agape love. It is the kind of love that gives not wanting anything in return. There are no conditions to meet to receive my love. With you that is now different. You are choosing to leave the relationship you had with me. Therefore you will no longer be a recipient of my love. Your nature now is that which, at its best, only gives in order to receive something in return. And when nothing in return is given, the result in you will always be anger. Anger is always the result of someone giving to another and expecting something in return. However, when the expectation of receiving something back in return doesn't happen, then anger is the result. Anger always comes from a blocked need. A woman, for example, who cooks her husband's favorite meal, will be angry at him if he doesn't acknowledge her effort to please him with at least a 'thank you'. An embrace or even a kiss would be better. However, in your case, you want the worship of mankind. That kind of worship occurs only if a man values the person being worshipped. In my case, my worshipper senses my love and desire to meet his or her needs. His sins and rebellion against me as God is turned into devotion when he understands and experiences my forgiveness. Man's thankfulness is the basis of his worship of me. When a person ceases being thankful, they no longer can be a worshiper of mine. You will never have that true worship. You won't ever experience true worship since you are not a loving and giving person. Since you have nothing meaningful to give, mankind will never be thankful to you. That is why you are now and forever will seek men to sin in rebellion against me. Since you cannot attain their worship, you don't want me to have theirs either. That is now what drives you. This desire for man's worship now compels you. You are overwhelmed with this desire to get mankind to sin. When they do, you are indirectly worshipped. For they choose you, instead of me. Mankind will not be conscious of this fact except for the fact they will feel shame and guilt when they do sin. Your plan to keep mankind from experiencing these feelings will be fruitful in some, but not all. You see, I too have a plan to remove shame and guilt from man's consciousness, should they ever sin."

Satan: "I can meet the needs of every person who will ever live. I have a plan in mind that will result in people's needs being met."

God: "You are completely wrong to believe people living to fulfill their needs 'in the flesh' will be satisfied. You equate Eros love, which I designed for men and women to enjoy within the bonds of marriage, as something that will satisfy mankind as they lust for one another. You think that mankind committing acts of fornication with each other will somehow satisfy the deep longings they will have for Agape love. Those acts temporarily satisfy mankind, but fail to envelop an individual with the kind of love only I can give them. People will tire of those activities, even after you persuade them to attempt different types of sexual activity. In addition to this, your plan to use the wealth people accumulate along with the goods that that wealth buys, to satisfy those deep longings for value will also fail. They will finally feel the futility of building esteem on the shifting sand of wealth. They will come to realize the truth of this Proverb: 'What does it profit a man if he gains the whole world, but loses his own soul?' Those that never realize this Proverb's truth will spend eternity with you in Hell."

Satan: "My plan for the future history of earth does not include me spending any time in Hell. Rather, I will be reigning with you as god of this earth. This will make mankind happy. They will prefer my rule over them as opposed to your rule. My rule will allow them freedom to do whatever they desire to do. Your law is too restrictive. When one lives without your restrictive laws, they are truly free and godlike."

God: "My laws allow mankind to experience joy knowing their behavior pleases me and constructs a basis for fellowship with me and worship of me. Adam and Eve enjoy our time together learning about me and the creative order I designed. They know I created them for myself and there is nothing I wouldn't do for them. They are beginning to understand the complexities of the building blocks of life. Already they are marveling at how the body works and how the food chain is designed to give health to their bodies."

Satan: "People do not need you to understand the things of this earth. All they have to do is study those things you made to figure out how they work."

God: "Don't you think deducing Intelligent Design is as good as having the Designer, himself, instruct you?"

Satan: "I am as good a teacher as you. And it is easy for me to figure out how you created and designed certain things. If providing explanations of things are essential to being God, I can do that as well, if not better, than you."

God: "If that is so, why not begin with an explanation of what has changed in your nature since I created you? Explain also how your thinking changed since you came to the conclusion you could be a god and manage this world as good as I."

Satan: "All I know is that from the feedback I was receiving from some of my fellow angels, they esteemed me to be more beautiful and intelligent than any of the other angels. They observed my work around your throne and thought I was as great as you. From that time on I realized the truth in what they were saying and I became excited as I formulated plans to live my life independent from you. Instead, now I can become the object of worship myself."

God: "When Adam and Eve worship me, it is because they find value in me. They are in awe of me. That I find joy being with them is exhilarating to them. They want to be like me in regards to my transitive attributes. Their response of praise signals a sincere appreciation for all that I am and my commitment to love them. There is now nothing in you worthy of praise. There is now nothing in your character of value that mankind would want to emulate. There is now nothing in you that would draw mankind to want to be like you or to seek you as their God. Nothing in you now exists or ever will exist that will create the desire in mankind to worship you and exalt what you now have become. You have completely changed from the wonderful angel I made you. Your

splendor brought glory to me as many angels expressed appreciation to me for what I had designed in you. They were amazed at my
creative genius evidenced in your angelic greatness. However, now
your pride has changed you from a person that serves to a person
that wants to be served. You no longer find value in me or the plans
I have for mankind. The plans I have for mankind to experience
peace and brotherhood throughout the nations of the world, you
have come to despise. You no longer desire to give, but rather to
receive. And when that need in you is not met, you will become
angry. Your anger will be the impetus behind slaughtering every
individual that loves and worships me instead of following your
shallow promises of prosperity. Much of what I have just said to
you is prophetic based on the idea of you being god." This hypo-
thetical conversation between God and Satan will continue in the
next Chapter.

Questions:

1. Why is it important that a Christian have a "world view" that includes the existence of Satan, the other fallen angels and those angels that still serve the Lord Jesus Christ?

_____

_____

_____

2. How would you associate the current pandemic known as Covid-19 and the wake of deaths it has produced, with the words of Jesus in John 8:44 describing Satan as a murderer?

_____

_____

_____

3. What characteristics of the Garden of Eden made it a "Paradise"?

_____

_____

_____

4. Jesus often instructed the disciples to "fear not". How is that possible?

_____

_____

_____

5. Read Psalm 119:105. Does the Word of God have this effect in your life?

_____

_____

_____

6. Has the thought mentioned in this Chapter, that sin, in essence, is an act of worshipping Satan, penetrated deeply into your soul? How?

    _____

    _____

    _____

7. What similarities exist between the temptation of Eve in Genesis Three and the temptations to sin you face? Are Satan's purposes the same?

    _____

    _____

    _____

8. In this deduced dialogue between God and Satan, what thoughts about Satan appear to be important as you "resist Satan", your adversary?

    _____

    _____

    _____

9. In this deduced conversation between God and Satan, what new information about God do you now understand? (Identify the Scriptures that support you thoughts)

    _____

    _____

    _____

Chapter Three

Satan: "It seems clear to me now that you are not disposed to give me the position of god over planet Earth."

God: "That is a correct analysis of what I just said to you. I will not share my glory with another created being. In the future my prophet Isaiah will make that abundantly clear. The Trinity is united by the characteristics we share. There is no way to include you into the fellowship we share. We are holy and you are not. You do not share in our Holiness. It is that which we desire for all mankind to experience in relationship with us. Your goals exist in opposition to our goals for mankind. To be clear, the answer is <u>no</u> for you to rule as god over this world."

Satan: "You interrupted me before I had a chance to complete my thought!"

God: "Yes, I know. Have you already forgotten I know what you are going to say before you verbalize your thoughts?"

Satan: "Then you know what I propose."

God: "Since you believe that you would be a better god than we are to Adam and Eve and subsequently to all the families of the Earth, you want to propose that we allow Adam and Eve to choose whom they want as their God. One of the things we endowed mankind with is a will. They can and will make choices throughout their lives on this planet. So we agree. Let the games begin. You stand before Adam and Eve and I will do the same. We will ask them to choose whom they want to be their God. They can then choose between you and us."

Satan: "No! That scenario you just mentioned is unfair to me. Under those conditions they would obviously choose you. You have spent time with them. They know you and have experienced your love and kindness. They do not know me."

God: "We will allow you to spend time with them so they can get to know you. However, do you really think they would pick you if they understood the nature behind the entity you have now become?"

Satan: "I am not proposing you in all your glory stand before them and I stand there dwarfed in comparison. That would be totally unfair to me."

God: "I know what you are going to propose, but I want you to say it."

Satan: "Of course, I would be glad to do that. You have spent time with Adam and Eve, so they know quite a bit about you. Therefore, I request that you not be there when they make their choice. You will be there in their memory of what you have said to them and with the evidence of who you are reflected in your creation which you have placed all around them. To make it fair, I too will camouflage myself. I will be represented there evidenced by the words I share with them."

God: "That is intelligent of you to refuse to appear before them as the entity you have become. They would recoil in your presence once they gleaned the truth about you. In fact, the next time we would meet in the Garden of Eden, they would ask me why I had created a being like you. Of course I would then have to explain that what they saw was not what I created. When I would explain what sin and pride can do to an individual, it would then make sense to them how you came into existence and how that now you exist as an enemy to the truth and to all that is good."

Satan: "Then we have a deal, right?"

God: "Yes. We do not want anyone to feel constrained to follow us and worship us against their will."

Satan: "I need you to affirm that if I am successful, you will not completely destroy Adam and Eve and start all over again with someone else. In fact, I need you to confirm that you will not destroy any of my work. If I am able to persuade Adam and Eve to choose me over you, I will become god of this world. As such, I have plans to create religious systems among mankind, wherever they choose to dwell. Those systems that I create will result in their worship of me. I want your assurance you will honor the choices made by mankind. You work among the people you choose to accomplish your will and I will work among the people I choose who are following my leadership."

God: "You have chosen the word "persuade" to describe your activity and the plan you have to tempt Eve and Adam to sin. The word persuade involves using truthful facts to convince someone of a right course of action, whether it is to convince a juror to vote guilty in a capital case based on the evidence of wrong doing by a perpetrator, or whether it is to convince Adam and Eve to eat the fruit I forbade them to eat. You will never persuade anyone to sin by using the truth about sin and what it does to destroy their own life and the lives of others. Instead your nature now is that which tries to manipulate people's behavior through lies. This is your nature now and it will mark the path you travel throughout history."

Satan: "You think you are so smart that you can see what the end of time will be like. However, I know this to be true. I will establish a "course for this world to follow that will satisfy the needs of people like Adam and Eve. (Ephesians 2:2-3) They will never know it is I who is orchestrating this earthly lifestyle they will be embracing."

God: "You are again wrong, Lucifer. First, I am God and as such I know the beginning from the ending. I am the Alpha and Omega. So allow me to teach you how your reign as god will come to an end if you are successful in your temptation of Eve. I have created a place for you and your deceiving angels in which you will spend eternity. Mankind will be the agency that will refuse your kingdom and call me back to establish mine. In so doing, I will keep my agreement with you to act in respect to what mankind wants. You will be judged by mankind, the very ones you led astray into sin. They will find you guilty of sinning against me and them. Your punishment will involve being thrown into a place called the Lake of Fire. This is a place which I created for you and all your rebellious angels. You will burn in the scorching fire of this place forever. Because your sin is against me, and because I am eternal, your retribution will be forever. Secondly, mankind will know all about you and your schemes. I will reveal those schemes to them and reveal how to gain the victory over them. Because we have agreed to only work through people, and for us not to reveal our glory as God directly in face to face meetings with mankind, I will choose a people through whom I will write down my instructions and reveal a way to escape your rule as god over them. To avoid violating our agreement with you, one of us will come to earth and take man's humanity and then tell the truth about you. He will reveal the plan I have for them and how mankind can become beneficiaries of this plan called Salvation. This plan of mine will result in our taking back what is rightfully ours by virtue of our creation. Thirdly, you and your fellow like-minded angels will not meet the deep longings people have since we created man in our "Image". However, we agree to let you try. We agree to what you are asking of us. You will be free to roam the world and continue to tempt mankind with the choice of either believing in us or the way of life you are proposing. However, we will oppose and undo any work you do that eliminates the free exercise of mankind's will. If you demonize anyone, you will have changed the agreement between us. If that happens, we will, along with our people, exorcise those demons working in that capacity. They will then make a quick exit into hell."

Satan: "Understood. Are you agreeing to work and bring your plans to fruition through individuals as I do the same? The only exception to that will be my temptation to Eve and Adam. Since there are no other individuals alive through whom I can work, then, with your permission, I choose to work through the most subtle creature you have made. Is that acceptable to you all?

God: "Yes it is. But since we will not impede your temptation by our personal presence,, it is necessary in this situation, that you reference the words that we have spoken to Adam."

Satan: "Any attempt on your part to take back what is mine, should I succeed in my temptation of Eve, will be met with the combined force and power that all of the angels under my command possess."

God: "From the foundations of the world we knew this would be your strategy. We knew before we created this universe and all that is in it, that you would rebel against us at a certain point in time. We further knew your rebellion would cause much pain and suffering for many people. However, the kind of love we share in the Trinity for each other we wanted to share with mankind. This was our motivation when we decided to create mankind. Our nature of love compels us to share that love with mankind who are created in our image. By virtue of that fact, mankind is capable of experiencing the kind of love we as God in Trinity share with each other. We knew mankind would thrive on this kind of love despite any difficulty they might experience."

Satan: "If you love Adam and Eve so much, why did you tell them they would 'die' if they violated your law related to eating from the tree of knowledge of good and evil? Why not give Adam and Eve a pass if I am successful in tempting them to sin? Let them stay in this beautiful garden you created for them. That would show them the love you speak of having for them."

God: "The unity we as God share in love is based on the fact that each one of us is holy. Holiness is the ruling attribute of ours that is used to govern our relationship with each other, and holiness is the same attribute we will use in governing the world. Should Adam and Eve sin they will no longer be without sin which will make them unholy. Therefore they will have to suffer the consequences should they sin. Fellowship with us will be broken should they sin so that we will not walk with them in this garden. In fact, this garden will no longer be their home. To experience our love in fellowship with us would require mankind to be like us in our holy nature. We therefore also have a plan for mankind to regain this righteous and holy condition that would be lost should Adam and Eve sin. Our plan would strip you and your fellow demons of the powers they possess. You are deceived in your thinking to believe you can stand against us, now or sometime in the future when we take back control of this world and reign over it. Like parents who would laugh at their small child trying to pick up a 50 lb. dumb-bell, so we will laugh at your feeble attempts to thwart the will of God from being done."

Satan: "Good luck in your attempts to take back what would be mine should my temptation of Eve and Adam work as I have planned."

God: "'Luck' when used with the word 'good' is a phrase you will teach mankind to use when in competition with each other. You will also teach mankind to use the phrase 'What luck' when they are successful in some kind of competition and are expressing their jubilance. However, the same golf ball putted on the same line and with the same speed under the same conditions as the previous shot will go into the same hole every time the putt is attempted. It doesn't depend on 'luck' to sink a putt as if a god called 'luck' will make it go into the hole on the green. For you to use that phrase with us is an insult to our intelligence. Anyone in the future who uses that term probably doesn't realize they are expressing a belief in a god called 'luck'. In the same way, for someone to state that 'they are lucky' is to really be saying that the god called 'luck' favors them. For you to use the term 'luck' reveals your finiteness and inability to think rationally. If you came to us for permission to test Adam and Eve and to see whom they wanted to be God over them, and knowing if you were successful, you would be the god of this world, why would you accept the idea of another god called 'luck' also ruling over the affairs of mankind alongside you?"

Satan: "Most people in the future will not think that deeply. In addition to that, if they think that there is god called 'luck', it will get them used to the idea of there being many gods, which eliminates the idea of there being just one God. You see, I am smarter than you thought."

God: "We know exactly how intelligent you are since we designed you and created you. Since you no longer are without sin, leave our presence. You are a disgusting and detestable angel."

Satan: "Before I leave, I want clarification on our agreement to allow mankind to choose what- ever actions they take without any interference on your part. We can attempt to influence their decisions, but cannot make their decisions for them."

God: "That is correct. However, any attempt on your part to invade or possess a person with the goal of making decisions on their behalf will be addressed by me or any of my Christian believers. We also work according to the will of our followers. Therefore, if any of my followers pray and ask me to do a certain thing, I will do it. I will not do anything that I am not asked to do. That is the definition of a perfect gentleman, something that has evaded your comprehension."

Satan left his audience with God and returned from the third heaven to Earth. He entered the Garden of Eden with the permission slip to be there which he attained from God. Though he indicated God's authority by asking Eve to recite what God had said concerning the abundance of trees in the garden from which she could eat, he did not overtly ask Adam and Eve to choose between God and himself as their choice of the God they wanted to rule over them. He hid the fact that to disobey what God had said was ultimately to choose Satan as their leader and god since they would be trusting in what he said as opposed to what God said. This principle is true of all people. To not follow God's law and instructions for life is to choose to follow Satan's, the god of this world. His directive that accompanies his temptation is always to not pay attention to what God has said in the Bible. Because Satan wants to remain god of this world, he and his angels tempt mankind to eliminate their dependence on the Bible. They know that they are worshipped as gods when they deceive mankind to trust in their own ways of living. They know mankind will live this way hiding from the shame of their sin by redefining truth. Satan takes glee in mankind's attempt to live without the feelings of guilt when they rationalize away the idea of sin by saying right and wrong are relative terms. When truth is made relative, mankind's sin nature is put on display.

The 'radical left' in our country today is trying to eliminate everything that relates to history, whether it is statues that recall the work of our founders or generals that fought for America's freedom in the Civil War. They want to eliminate Christmas related themes from our front yards and the Ten Commandments from our courthouses. They want to eliminate any words describing gender since the Bible says "God created them male and female". They want to eliminate God from our culture. They are now attacking the First Amendment which guarantees the right of churches to exist and worship God. These are but a few examples of an orchestrated plan to eliminate the worship of God in our country. What the radical left does not understand is that with every successful attempt at removing our heritage, they are in essence, worshipping Satan. They are taking us back into the Garden of Eden and asking us to choose "which God do you want to serve as your God."

Notice that when Eve was asked by Satan exactly what God had said concerning their daily menu that she incorrectly recited what God had said. She said to Satan, "We may eat from the trees in the garden, but 'you must not eat from the tree in the middle of the garden, and you musts not touch it, or you will die'". (Genesis

3:2-3) God never said they could not touch the Tree of Knowledge of Good and Evil or the fruit on it. Adam and Eve added the idea of "never touching it." I presume they did this to put an extra boundary around the tree so that they would not eat from it. What they did is called "legalism" in our day. It is the placing of a law we create and then imposing it upon ourselves. The motive in so doing is to keep us from breaking one of God's laws so we do not sin. Christians do the same thing today. For example, Ephesians 5:18 is written by the Apostle Paul to the Church composed of Christian believers. These Jesus followers were instructed in this verse "not to be drunk with wine which leads to debauchery." Legalists, hoping to keep from being drunk, established a law that it was a sin to drink alcohol. This is a manmade law since it is not a law God gave to mankind to observe. Drinking wine is itself not a sinful activity. In fact, The Apostle Paul wrote to Timothy to "stop drinking water only, but also a little wine" (1 Timothy 5:23) for medicinal purposes. The purpose of Paul's admonition is to keep the Christian from activities described as debauchery. The word "Debauchery" describes the shameful activity of people who feel released from any and all prohibitions. Alcohol is a depressant and when it is in our bloodstream, it suppresses the thoughts of the mind. When in a drunken state, a person has no fears or concerns because the mind is no longer alerting them that danger is near. That is why a drunken person may jump off a bridge or walk in front of a moving car. In a bar, for example, a drunken person might say and do things normally they would not say or do. They might be married, but that would not keep them from trying to pick up another person with whom they could commit an act of infidelity. In a drunken state, people share things they normally would keep a secret. However, there is the sense no one will remember what was said the next day, so drunken people become great conversationalists in a bar. In that sense their conversations are therapeutic since they can "confess their sins to one another." Drunkenness puts our morality on shifting sands. Therefore the Apostle Paul says be careful when drinking wine. Do not do so to excess so that you become drunk. Jesus said "It is not what goes into a man's mouth that makes him 'unclean', but what comes out of his mouth makes him 'unclean.'" (Matthew 15:11) In other words, when drunk, one may say things or do things they could later regret.

Legalism leads people to focus on the laws they make, not the heart of the supreme lawgiver himself. That in turn leads people away from a true worship of God. Instead they focus on their behavior that conforms to their own laws, not the law of God or the heart of God, who prescribed the laws. They never, under the condition of legalism, repent of their own behavior, because they are the ones who created the law. Since they are not god, there is no authority behind their own laws. It is only sin committed against the true lawgiver of which we are to repent. Therefore legalism focuses only on our own behavior that meets the conditions of our own laws. Therefore, we never feel the guilt from sin that would drive us to our knees before the Savior of the World who died for them. This is why Jesus said of the religious people of his own time, "These people honor me with their lips, but their hearts are far from me. They worship me in vain; their teachings are but rules taught by men." (Matthew 15:8-9) When Satan spotted this weakness in Eve evidenced by legalism, he knew it was a simple step to deceive her into believing the lie. The lie Satan told Eve is this: "you do not need to depend on God or what he says because you will not die." That statement was just the opposite of what God had said. However, she already had established a law independent of what God said, so why not believe the serpent, even though it also was against what God said. She had already done the same thing. Therefore she was vulnerable to deception, and thus the committing of sin.

Every Christian needs to examine their thinking while looking for any legalism they might have embraced. If it is there, Satan's deception will soon ensue. The temptation will be to violate the law established in my legalistic condition. However, since I have become like god by making my own laws, there is no guilt in breaking them since "I have become like God!" In this sense, Satan was correct in telling Eve that she "would become like God." In the next Chapter, Satan's activities after "the fall" until the Flood will be unveiled.

Questions:

1. I was raised in a legalistic church and family. We were told we couldn't go to movies, drink, smoke, dance or play cards. What sort of legalistic ideas were you told to observe?

_____

_____

2. I once heard a former Dallas Theological Seminary professor tell of legalistic teaching in his background. He said it once tormented his thinking. Is there any legalistic thinking in your background that causes you consternation about your activities as a Christian?

_____

_____

3. After taking my first church as a pastor, one of the members said to me that if he heard that I had ever taken a drink of alcohol, he would work to have me fired. What is legalistic about that statement made to me?

_____

_____

4. Were you aware that every time you sin you ultimately are worshipping Satan? Explain why this is a new thought to you or perhaps why you disagree with it.

_____

_____

_____

5. Were you aware that a dialogue between Satan and God had occurred before Satan appeared in the Garden of Eden with Eve? After reading this dialogue, what information stands out to you?

_____

_____

_____

6. The statements made by God in this dialogue can be traced back to statements made by Jesus recorded in the Gospels. What in the dialogue reminded you of truths recorded in the Gospels?

_____

_____

_____

7. What in the dialogue reminded you of what Jesus said recorded in John 14:1-2? Especially focus on the phrase "that where I am, there you may be also."

_____

_____

_____

8. How does God's ruling attribute of holiness make sense of what we find recorded on the pages of history?

_____

_____

_____

9. How is the question posed to Adam and Eve about who they wanted to serve as God similar to the question Pilate asked the people at Jesus' trial whether to release Barabbas or Jesus?

_____

_____

_____

Chapter Four

The Book of Job is thought by Biblical scholars to be the oldest book in the Bible. The book begins with Satan roaming the earth and taking inventory of the work he and his fallen angels had accomplished. By the time the Book of Job opens, there are probably millions and millions of people alive and living on the earth. Satan comes from roaming the earth since the earth is now under his control as god. He is not omniscient, so he has to wander the earth to know what is happening. He is not omnipresent, so he has to travel personally to take inventory of what his angels are accomplishing. He is keeping watch over the populations that then existed on earth. In Bishop Ussher's Seventeenth Century Chronology, he wrote there were 1656 years between Adam and Eve's sin in the Garden of Eden and the flood. He wrote that more than 500 million people could have been alive prior to the Flood. Given the Biblical record that people then were living between 700 and 960 years, there would have been millions of people alive by virtue of procreation. It is not important whether you embrace this exact time table developed by Bishop Ussher. And if it be so that another thousand years or more pinpoint the exact time of God's creation, so be it. The point here is that many people were alive prior to the flood and Satan would have been active doing work among them, a work reflective of his nature. He would be lying to people and deceiving them as they began cities and cultures. He would be actively inaugurating new religious systems that would lead adherents to worship him. He rightly believed that everyone who followed the religious systems he designed would be sinning against the true God of the Bible and thereby, would be worshipping him. For in the Ten Commandments mankind is instructed to have no other gods other than the Creator God.

Satan's scheme was to create a belief system that would eliminate their feelings of guilt which emanated from the presence of the Image of God in them, namely their sense of morality and their conscience attached to it. Satan's plan was to erase guilt consciousness in man. He did so in people primarily by erecting sacrificial systems in their religions that released them from guilt. Without guilt and shame they would not seek the true God for release from it. This was Satan's desire when he had his audience with God and it will continue to be his desire throughout history. He wants to remain god of this world and enjoy the worship he receives from mankind.

The Book of Job has recorded that when Satan came from "roaming the world", he arrived before God and was asked by God what he thought of his servant Job. This question reveals that Satan's strategy was not working on everyone. Job had escaped the temptation to worship other gods and was steadfast in his worship of the true Creator God, Elohim. Satan's pride would not allow him to accept the premise that he failed in reference to Job. Satan therefore tried to avoid the fact of his failure to seduce Job. He blamed Job's decision to worship God as opposed to himself on the fact that God maneuvered Job to worship him by the blessings he had given to Job. Adam and Eve played the "blame game" when confronted by God of their sin. The "left" today blames former president Trump for everything under the sun. All the "left" news agencies refuse to admit fault when their lies are exposed. Satan is no different. He refused to take ownership of his failure as it related to Job. Satan's response was an indication of his pride. He said Job would curse God to his face if the blessings God had provided were taken away from him. In essence, Satan said Job was a "rice" (a term coined by missionaries) believer only because God had provided so much for him. In other words, Job was in this relationship with God in order to get something out of it. Satan said Job was God's worshipper only because of what God gave materially and physically to him. Therefore God allowed Satan to remove God's blessings on Job to prove Satan's statement was a lie. As Satan removed God's blessings on Job, Job continued to remain faithful in his worship of God. Job said, "Naked I came from my mother's womb, and naked I will depart. The Lord gave and the Lord has taken away; may the name of the Lord be praised." (Job 1:21-22) In essence Job said that what the Lord God gave him by virtue of their fellowship together was more meaningful than anything that had been taken from him. Because of this reality Job was experiencing with God, and which is available to all mankind, Satan has had to work all that much harder to hide this truth declared by the words of Job. However, Satan cannot fill the deep longings mankind has in their souls. Job had those longings and God fulfilled them. Job had learned that the God-shaped vacuum he had in his life could only be satisfied by God. Satan has tried to keep that truth from all mankind. He constantly is at work trying to persuade mankind to replace the choice of God with the substitutes he provides in his world system. (Ephesians 2:1-3) These substitutes do not satisfy mankind's souls. The psalmist understood this and wrote, "Delight yourself in the Lord and he will give you the desires of your heart." The Book of Hebrews declared Moses understood the reality Job experienced with God and enjoyed it himself. The Bible declared Moses also chose God over the earthly pleasures offered by Satan. It is written of Moses that "He chose to be mistreated along with the people of God rather than enjoy the pleasures of sin for a season." (Hebrews 11:25) Solomon tried all the things this world had to offer to meet the deep longings for God in his life and wrote, "Meaningless! Meaningless!" says the teacher. "Everything is meaningless!" (Ecclesiastes 12:8) In other words, substitutes do not work!

The Book of Enoch recorded that prior to the flood, fallen angels procreated with women who in turn gave birth to a group of people called Nephilim. The Bible also mentions the Nephilim. It recorded the following about them: "The Nephilim were on the earth in those days, and also afterward, when the sons of God went to the daughters of men and had children by them. They were the heroes of old, men of renown." (Genesis 6:4) The Book of Enoch is not a part of the Old Testament Canon and therefore is not to be regarded as Scripture. We are not to take anything written in it as from God. There are, however, a couple of things needing to be scrutinized concerning what is written in the Book of Enoch. First, the group called Nephilim received their name from the Hebrew word "Naphal". The word means to "fall upon" as when someone robs or rapes another person restricting their rights like the ones we have under the Constitution of the United States. These were evil individuals. The MS13 group of illegals that have illegally come to live in our country are like the Nephilim who existed in the time prior to the Flood. Recall that in Genesis 6:5, God is said to have witnessed the deeds of the Nephilim, and "saw how great man's wickedness on the earth had become, and that every inclination of the thoughts of his heart were only evil all the time." Therefore he thought to use the flood to destroy them.

Secondly, notice the phrase "sons of God". The author of the Book of Enoch wrote that this phrase was used to describe fallen angels. Even though "universal mythologies" described "God-men" coming from the stars, there is no evidence to equate them as the "sons of God" mentioned in the Bible. My Hebrew professor at Trinity University was Dr. Walter Kaiser. He taught this phrase was used to describe an upper level of society that existed in antediluvian times. This upper class gained their positions by what means no one knows for sure, except to say they had children with the women of their time. It is natural that a man and women, after engaging in sexual copulation, create the condition within a woman called pregnancy. After a nine month gestation period, a pregnant woman will give birth to the child she is carrying in her womb. That is what is being described here in Genesis Six. Men from an upper class of society called "sons of God" were having sexual intercourse with the beautiful women of their time. That these beings having sex with the beautiful women of their time were "fallen angels" doesn't make any sense. The reason it makes no sense is because angels do not have bodies like human beings. Jesus was asked a question about a woman who had had seven husbands all who died during her lifetime. The question was "which husband would be hers in heaven?" Jesus' answer makes it clear that there is no sexuality associated with the heavenly bodies that will be given to Christians during their existence in heaven. 1 Corinthians 15 provides us with further details of what our new heavenly bodies will be like. However, concerning our current discussion about our future bodies, Jesus said, "You will be like the angels". (Mark 12:25) In the Bible angels are not described anatomically as is mankind. In other words, there are not men and women angels. There is no sexual expression between them. This is a difficult idea to wrap our heads around since I, as the author, and you the reader, are human beings characterized Biblically as either male or female. Males and females have sexual desires that are characterized by those genetic impulses that lead to sexual activity. That is the way God designed us sexually. However, he didn't design this similarity into angels. Therefore the Nephilim are not the children of male angels who had intercourse with women here on earth. One may argue that these angels had the ability to appear in the form of a human being and that was how they were able to have intercourse with women. To this objection I would answer that it is God who designed our bodies and made them capable of sexual activity. Satan and his angels do not have the creative genius and power to duplicate God's sexual design that would eventuate in procreation with women. They had no omniscience to make a sperm and a way of depositing it in a woman, whereby allowing that sperm to unite with a woman's egg.

There has been much written and many myths proposed to describe antediluvian culture. Plato, for example, believed in the Egyptian legend of Atlantis. Herodotus wrote of the existence of another Egyptian legend about the continent of Hyperborea in the far north, the capital city of which was Ultima Thule. Other legends speak of the four lost continents. Nordic legends speak of blue-eyed blond "gods" that influenced the later ideology of Nazi Germany. The Bible speaks of a water canopy around the earth that provided a Green-house effect in the atmosphere. The Bible recorded this in Genesis 1:6, "And God said, 'Let there be an expanse between the waters to separate water from water." The Apostle Peter also referred to this fact of creation when he wrote that people "deliberately forget that long ago by God's word the heavens existed and the earth was formed out of water and by water." (2 Peter 3:5) This canopy, among other things, caused a warm uniform temperature to exist on this planet. Instead of the snow-packed North and South Poles that exist now, these places would have been covered with plush vegetation. The earth would have been a much different place to live. This phenomenon was caused by a much different weather pattern that then existed on this planet. This was made possible by the warm uniform temperature on the Earth caused by the water canopy. That is why credence should be given to Herodotus' statement of an existence of a city in the "far north". The fact that many vast oil and gas reserves have been found in the far north regions of the earth and beyond the coasts of the continents reveal dense vegetation once existed there. This vegetation came under extreme pressure caused by the depths of the waters of the Flood that were higher than the highest mountains that existed on this planet. Psalm 104:6-8 states this about God's creation, "You covered the earth with the deep as with a garment; the waters stood above the mountains." Every continent has mountains covered with sedimentary rock. Those sedimentary rocks have been found to have sea life fossils in them. The only way these fossils were buried under sedimentary rock was by a flood. That water pressure created the oil and gas preserves which now have been discovered on this planet. The fact that some of these preserves are found off the coasts of continents proves the data found in the Biblical account of the Flood, namely that the earth was once covered with less water than it is now. This accounts for the shelf found offshore from the beaches proving that at one time the shore was further out than it is now. The change is due to the excess water that came down from what once existed as a water canopy around the earth. This excess water created new coast lands on the continents.

During the existence of this water canopy, no detrimental radiation would have penetrated the earth's atmosphere. The results of this condition are noteworthy. People would have lived longer. There would not have been skin cancer. Vegetables would have grown much larger than they do today. Experiments have been done on vegetables grown in protected areas where ultraviolet radiation was restricted. The results were amazing: 150 lb. pumpkins, 40 lb. tomatoes, etc.

During the Antediluvian Period, mankind was busy building massive architectural monuments. These edifices are investigated on the History Chanel on a show entitled "Ancient Aliens." The authors of the show have continued asking the question whether the civilizations responsible for building these massive structures were aided by visitors from another planet. Their conclusions are based on the fact that what was built could not have been built by normal human beings. The technology needed was not in existence at this time. Massive stones, weighing 200 tons and larger were cut to exact lengths and then placed perfectly to fit into stone structures. This architectural achievement was beyond the capabilities of mankind. Therefore they concluded these ancient civilizations had help from these ancient aliens. Scalar technology based on the theory of a fourth dimension where powerful energies can be transferred into our reality and change it cannot be the answer. However, even as I write this, I could be wrong. I do not know the limits God placed on Satan's power and abilities. Perhaps Satan had available to him Scalar technology so that he and his fallen demons, masquerading as god-men from outer space, aided these ancient civilizations in building these edifices. The authors of the show "Ancient Aliens" conclude that visitors from another world were behind these architectural achievements, but they do not explain how or by what means these edifices were built. The main point of the show was that the authors of the show, "Ancient Aliens," attributed this prowess to visitors from another world. They have help in their conclusions from literature like the Sumerian Flood myth that reported a time when the gods in the universe walked the earth with humans.

Another more plausible solution to how these edifices were built is found in the Apostle Peter's description of angels recorded in 2 Peter 2:11. He wrote of angels that they were "stronger and more powerful" than mankind. Through their powers of levitation they could have moved these massive stones into place, much like what was depicted in the "Star Wars" series of films. In that popular series, the "dark side", led by Darth Vader, was attempting to destroy the Jedi and those leading the "resistance" against them. During the various films, the powers of this resistance were on display. Those powers were on display as the Jedi used the powers of "The Force." In one episode of the film, "The Empire Strikes back", "The Force" was used by Yoda to levitate a large object like Luke Skywalker's aircraft. Knowledge of this kind of power existed among civilizations prior to and after the Flood. In the Gilgamesh

Epic, a piece of literature written to explain the Flood, the word "deep" is used and translated meant "unknown mysteries". The Bible alludes to the existence of "unknown mysteries" when it tells of the ability of Egyptian religious leaders who turned their staffs into snakes like Moses did his. The Bible directly forbids God's people from investigating the "secret things." Deuteronomy 29:29 declared "The secret things belong to the Lord our God, but the things revealed belong to us and our children, forever, that we may follow all the words of the law."

Another reason to ascribe credit to "fallen angels" for this work among mankind is that what they helped man build were temples for the worship of gods, themselves included. This is what Satan wanted for himself and the fallen angels who rebelled against God. Deuteronomy 32:15-17 supports this statement by these recorded words describing a man named Jeshurun, "He abandoned the God who made him and rejected the Rock his Savior. They made him (God) jealous with their foreign gods and angered him with their detestable idols. They sacrificed to demons, which are not God—gods they had not known, gods that recently appeared, gods your fathers did not fear." This is what Satan wanted when he decided to "raise his throne above God's" (Isaiah 14). His pride dictated that he should be the one worshipped. He convinced a number of other angels that mankind should worship them since they were superior in strength and mental prowess. They rebelled against the fact that they were to assist mankind by "ministering" to them. (Hebrews 1:14) Therefore Satan helped mankind build these "temples" in which they could worship these demons according to the religions Satan designed for them to observe. And this was his Modus Operandi exhibited in the past and will continue until he is thrown into "the Lake of Fire". This final abode of Satan is further described as "a lake of burning Sulfur" where he will be tormented day and night forever and ever. (Revelation 20:10)

Pictures of these ancient aliens are carved into the stones and rocks where these temples were constructed. These temples were built at different sites around the world. Though they were thousands of miles removed from each other, the pictures of these aliens inscribed there all bear a similar resemblance to each other. These are demons masquerading as gods with their pictures tattooed on the sides of these temples they helped erect. Just recently our government released its report on U.F.O.s. There were no definitive findings or explanations as to what these aircraft were or who was flying them. The sightings seem to indicate an image like a flying saucer. It makes sense to me that these visual sightings of Unidentified Flying Objects are the work and production of demons. The fact that they have done nothing to harm mankind, in my mind, proves only that they are not allowed by God to do anything else but appear and cause consternation. I believe later in history when the false prophet does miracles and brings signs to the people of the world, and uses those abilities to gain the allegiance of nations and people groups, that the beast and false prophet will say they are in control of the Unidentified Flying Objects. The Ancient Alien's show thought these visitors from outer space might have come from Pleiades or Orion. (Job 9:9)

After the Flood recorded in the Bible, Satan continued his work among the new civilizations that formed in various cities. His work paralleled much like what he did during the Antediluvian days. He created religions among people groups by deceiving them into thinking they were worshipping the true God, as opposed to a fake, want-to-be god. An extra-Biblical account of the Flood was found in the library of Ashurbanipal located in Nineveh called the Gilgamesh Epic. This Epic is but another example of Satan's work attempting to lead people away from the truth found in the Bible to man-made myths. There are some similarities between the Biblical account of the Flood and the story found in the Gilgamesh Epic. In the Bible, it took Noah 100 years to build the Ark, whereas in the

Gilgamesh Epic it only took Utnapishtim 7 days. In the Bible it rained 40 days while it rained only 7 in the Gilgamesh Epic.

The story line in the Gilgamesh Epic depicts a king named Utnapishim who reigned over the city of Shuruppak. He was chosen by the god Enki to survive the great flood. He and his wife gained immortality and a place among the gods for his work. Gilgamesh was king over Uruk who had a friend named Enkidu who helped him reduce his evil activities, one of which was the rape of women he fancied. When his friend Enkidu died, Gilgamesh, said to be part man and part god, was reminded of his mortality and went looking for Utnapishim, hoping that he could aid him in getting eternal life as well. Utnapishim told him of a plant that could give eternal life, but counseled him to abandon his search and live the rest of his life as a happy mortal. This story reflects the work of Satan after the Flood. He continued to raise up false religious systems that reflected the wishes of Utnapishim.

Archaeologists, described as people who dig up dirt on others (Ha Ha), have uncovered many ancient civilizations that reveal Satan's work among them. The evidence of that fact is that these civilizations worshipped false gods and built temples in which they could worship those gods. Some of those civilizations discovered were the Incan, Aztec, Persian, Greek, Chinese, Mayan, Egyptian, Indus Valley and Mesopotamian. The Romans worshiped Jupiter (Zeus), Juno and Minerva. They sacrificed animals having the same sex as the god they were worshipping. White animals were sacrificed to the gods of the upper world while black animals were sacrificed to the gods of the under-world. The Egyptian gods represented aspects of nature. Amun-Ra was the king of gods and goddesses. Osirus was the god of the after-life. Ra was the sun god. The Nile River was a god and when Moses, under the direction of God, turned it red, the meaning of which was quite clear. Their god had died. Each of the miracles performed by God and orchestrated through Moses and Aaron, revealed the superiority of Moses' God over the gods of Egypt.

The point of this Chapter was to trace Satan's activities after he left the Garden of Eden. There he received the right to rule this world as its god because of the sin of Adam and Eve. Armed with this authority, Satan initiated false religious systems among the civilizations formed during the years after Adam and Eve sinned. Those religious systems were designed not only to hide the existence of the true God but also to establish a system of worship that gave allegiance to Satan. The goal of his activity in history continues to be the same. He claims the worship of the world through the religions he has established. Satan's desire for the worship of the world will continue to evidence itself in the historicity of this planet. Unfolding before our very eyes, will be his continued attempt to gain worship by deceiving people to sin. The existence of abortion clinics are evidence of his work. The teaching of evolution is yet further evidence that he has been working. Getting the intellectual community to embrace the Critical Race Theory and teach it in the classrooms of the world is another of his deceptive accomplishments. The Devil aggressively seeks to erase the Scriptural fact that all men are created in the Image of God. He despises God and wants to eliminate evidence of his existence wherever he finds it.

Questions:

1. How does the information in this Chapter assist you in developing a correct world view?

   _____

   _____

   _____

2. Are able to ascertain the intensity of Satan's work as he worked in the past history of this world to erect false religious systems designed to bring him worship? Explain.

   _____

   _____

   _____

3. How does, in the "Star War" movies, the use of the phrase "The Force Be With You," find a parallel theme in the false religions Satan has designed?

   _____

   _____

   _____

4. Why would Satan inspire someone to write the Gilgamesh Epic?

   _____

   _____

5. What impressions did you have of Gilgamesh Epic?

   _____

   _____

   _____

6. Are you convinced that the creatures known as "ancient aliens" are simply demons masquerading as gods to achieve their goal of mankind's worship of them? Why or why not?

_____

_____

_____

7. Do you think there are similarities today of UFO sightings and the stories of Ancient Aliens from the past?

_____

_____

8. Do you agree with the interpretation given here about the identity of "the Sons of God" in Genesis 6:1ff? Explain

_____

_____

_____

9. What do you think are the "Secret things" mentioned in Deuteronomy 29:29?

_____

_____

_____

Chapter Five

C hapters 9-11 of Genesis depict the repopulation of the earth by the sons of Noah. Those four Chapters take us from immediately after the flood to the time of the covenant God made with Abraham recorded in Genesis Twelve. The covenant with Abraham informs the rest of the Old Testament and explains God's plan to remove Satan as god of this earth. Genesis 9-11 is important because it describes the why and how concerning the blessings of Noah to his three sons. In turn, those blessings explain the genealogies of Noah's sons and where they settled on this earth, and how those genealogies would relate to how the world was populated.

Genesis 9 begins with Noah planting a vineyard and one day becoming drunk with the wine produced from the grapes harvested from those vines. In his drunken state, he lay naked in his tent. The youngest brother, Ham, saw his father's nakedness and did something to his father. We know that he did something because the Bible states that "When Noah awoke from his wine and found out what his youngest son had done to him..." Exactly what he had done is speculative, except to say a hint to what happened may be learned from what occurred to Lot when he became drunk recorded in Genesis 19:30-38. In that text there was no Erectile Dysfunction (ED) when the daughters of Lot became pregnant by their father while he was drunk. If Ham did something similar to Noah's erection while drunk, that may account for the loss of moral decency and honor that one is to give to a parent (Fifth Commandment). The other two brothers, Shem and Japheth, did not want to see their father naked. So they covered him by walking backward with a covering, possibly a blanket or sheet, so they would not see their father naked. (Genesis 9:23)

Of special interest is the event described in Genesis 9 concerning the nakedness of Noah and how that affected the specific blessings given to each of the sons of Noah by their father. Ham and his son Canaan received no blessing. Rather a curse was given when Noah said "Servant of servants let him become to his brothers." (Genesis 9:25) In Tyndale's Old Testament Commentaries, author Derek Kidner wrote this about Noah's curse on Ham and Canaan: "That the curse fell on Canaan, youngest son of the offender, emphasizes its reference to Ham's succession rather than his person. For his breach of the family, his own family would falter. Since it confines the curse to this one branch within the Hamites, those who reckon the Hamite people in general to be doomed to inferiority have therefore misread the Old Testament as well as the New Testament." In his Commentary on the Old Testament, Keil Delitzsch reinforces this conclusion. He wrote, "Although this curse was expressly pronounced upon Canaan alone, the fact that Ham had no share in Noah's blessing, either for himself or his other sons, was a sufficient proof that his whole family was included by implication in the curse, even if it was to fall chiefly upon Canaan. And history confirms this supposition. The Canaanites were partly exterminated, and partly subjugated to the lowest form of slavery, by the Israelites who belonged to the family of Shem; and those who still remained were reduced by Solomon to the same condition (1 Kings 9:20-21)." The author continued to examine the curse on Canaan and wrote, "The Phoenicians, along with the Carthaginians and the Egyptians, who all belonged to the family of Canaan, were subjugated by the Japhetic Persians, Macedonians and Romans; and the remainder of the Hamitic tribes either shared the same fate, or still sigh, like the negroes, for example, and other African tribes, beneath the yoke of the most crushing slavery." Author Derek Kidner, Whom we cited earlier, wrote concerning Genesis 9:25-28, "Of the three oracles, only that on Shem uses God's personal name Yahweh; the significance of the fact begins to emerge at Genesis 12:1 and will dominate the Old Testament. Since Shem means 'name' there may well be a play on words here. The phrase 'Blessed be the Lord, the God of Shem' suggests that Shem is himself already in a covenant with Jahweh." The promise to Abraham that "all of the nations on earth will be blessed through him" (Genesis 12:1) is the fulfillment of the oracle pronounced on Shem by Noah. And the pronouncement on Japheth of enlarging lands and the nations filling those lands and a residing in the tents of Shem, finds fulfillment in Ephesians 3:4-6, "In reading this, then, you will be able to understand my insight into the mystery of Christ, which was not made known to men in other generations as it has now been revealed by the Spirit to God's holy apostles and prophets. This mystery is that through the Gospel the Gentiles are heirs together with Israel, members together of one body, and sharers together of the promise in Christ Jesus."

In Genesis 10, the three families of Noah are examined more closely. Ham and Japheth are dealt with first, leaving the rest of the book of Genesis to explore the lineage of Shem. The sons of Japheth, recorded in Genesis 10: 2-4, are said to dwell as far west as the Aegean to the area around the Caspian Sea. They stretch their territory north to Gog, Magog and Meschech (Ezekiel 38:2,6). In addition to that, Madai probably references the Medes who settled west of the Caspian Sea. Javan speaks to the Iconians, a branch of the Greeks, and the Scythians inhabiting Cyprus. A further study of the settlement of the sons of Noah can be found in Chapter 15 of Gleason Archer, Jr.'s book, "A Survey of Old Testament Introduction." In Genesis 11, God recorded the different languages given to people groups as they then spread themselves out over the world. As they go, they take with them the experiences of the three sons of Noah during and after the Flood and the role and character of God associated with those events. In explaining the association of the three sons of Noah in populating the earth, God is revealing how he took the knowledge of himself to the very peoples of the earth Satan is trying to deceive. The battle for the worship of mankind between Satan and God unfolds on the pages of history from Genesis 11 onward.

God's plan to redeem mankind is revealed in the Abrahamic Covenant recorded in Genesis 12:1-3. Abram is a descendant of Shem. Noah's blessing on Shem is fulfilled in the words recorded in the Old Testament. That blessing begins with God choosing Abraham to fulfill the words God spoke to Satan recorded in Genesis 3:15. There God said to Satan, "And I will put enmity between you and the woman, and between your offspring and hers; he will crush your head, and you will strike his heel." History records the aftermath of that enmity. However, not to be missed in Genesis 3:15 is the promise of God to "crush" the authority of Satan as god over this world. God said a "he" would come forth from a woman who would accomplish this "crushing". That "he" would be Jesus Christ. The Bible recorded how that "crushing" occurred in Colossians 2:15, "And having disarmed the powers and authorities, he made a public spectacle of them, triumphing over them by the cross."

How God would bring this "he" into the world began with this promise God gave to Abram, "Leave your country, your people and your father's household and go to the land I will show you. I will make you into a great nation and I will bless you; I will make your name great, and you will be a blessing. I will bless those who bless you and whoever curses you I will curse; and all peoples on the earth will be blessed through you." (Genesis 12:1-3) All the Old Testament prophets looked forward to the fulfillment of this promise to bring the "he" into the world. Some gave specific facts to identify the child that would be born of a woman. Moses said he would be Jewish, born in the lineage of Abraham. The promise that was given Abraham was passed on to his first born son, Isaac. Moses later wrote that the "he" would not come through the lineage of Esau, the first-born of Isaac. Rather, the Messiah, the "he", would be included in the genealogy of Jacob. Esau sold his birthright to Jacob revealing the lack of importance he gave to God's plan for bringing Salvation to mankind. This is why Scriptures record God hated Esau. (Malachi 1:3) The blessing and promise to bring Salvation to mankind passed from Jacob to one of his twelve sons. Jacob gave the blessing to Judah, marking the path of the genealogy of the "he". It began with Jacob, the grandson of Abraham, who said to Judah, "Judah, your brothers will praise you; your hand will be on the neck of your enemies; your father's sons will bow down before you. You are a lion's cub. O Judah, you return from the prey, my son. Like a lion he crouched and lies down, like a lioness—who dares to rouse him? The scepter will not depart from Judah, nor the ruler's staff from between his feet, until he comes to whom it belongs and the obedience of the nations..."

Later, the lineage of the "he" passed through the person David. (Luke 3:31) God had chosen him to be king over Israel and made a promise to him recorded in 2 Samuel 7 and 1 Chronicles 17:10. The prophet Nathan was told to tell David the following: "I declare to you that the Lord will build a house for you: When your days are over and you go to be with your fathers, I will raise up your offspring to succeed you, one of your own sons, and I will establish his kingdom. He is the one who will build a house for me, and I will establish his throne forever. I will be his father, and he will be my son. I will never take my love away from him, as I took it away from your predecessor. I will set him over my house and my kingdom forever; his throne will be established forever." The "he" was to be a part of the lineage of David and would fulfill the promise given to Abraham.

The story of the actual birth of the "he", is recorded in the Gospels of Mathew and Luke. The "he" was named Jesus, as instructed by the angel who appeared to Joseph (Matthew 1:18-25. In Matthew 1:17, the Bible declares, "Thus there were fourteen generations from Abraham to David, fourteen from David to the exile in Babylon, and fourteen from the exile to the Christ." Matthew's genealogy differs from Luke's genealogy in that Matthew's genealogy traces David's genealogy through his firstborn son of Bathsheba, wife of Solomon, while Luke's gospel traces David's genealogy through Nathan, David's literal firstborn son. The genealogy of Matthew traces the promise given to Abraham to Joseph through Solomon while the genealogy recorded in the Gospel of Luke traces the promise given to Abraham through Nathan to Mary. Since both Mary and Joseph are firstborns in their lineage, and since the promise is given to their firstborn son, Jesus, can be the only person who can be the fulfillment of the promise. Therefore Jesus is rightfully the Son of David, being the firstborn through both Nathan and Solomon. Jesus therefore is the one who can rightfully sit on David's throne forever as King of Kings and Lord of Lords. He has the physical right to sit on that throne through Nathan and the legal right to sit on that throne through Solomon (2 Samuel 7). Jesus is the only one in history who can fulfill the promise to David by God. The Apostle Paul recognizes this fact when he wrote to the churches in Galatia. In Galatians 3 it is recorded, "The Scripture foresaw that God would justify the Gentiles by faith, and announced the gospel in advance to Abraham. 'All nations will be blessed through you.' So those who have faith are blessed along with Abraham, the son of faith." (Galatians 3:8-9) Later in that same Chapter, the Apostle Paul wrote, "He redeemed us in order that the blessing given to Abraham might come to the Gentiles through Jesus Christ, so that by faith we might receive the promise of the Spirit." (Galatians 3:14) Later he again wrote, "If you belong to Christ, then you are Abraham's seed, and heirs according to the promise." (Galatians 3:29)

To the Christians at Rome, the Apostle Paul amplified and explained further these words written to the churches in Galatia. That amplification and explanation is recorded In Romans 4:13ff, "It was not through law that Abraham and his offspring received the promise that he would be heir of the world, but through the righteousness that comes by faith. For if those who live by law are heirs, faith has no value and the promise is worthless, because law brings wrath. And where there is no law, there is no transgression. Therefore, the promise comes by faith, so that it may be by grace and may be guaranteed to all Abraham's offspring---not only to those who are of the law but also to those who are of the faith of Abraham. He is the father of us all. As it is written, 'I have made you a father of many nations.' He is our father in the sight of God, in whom he believed---the God who gives life to the dead and calls things that are not as though they were."

Against all hope, Abraham in hope believed and so became the father of many nations, just as it had been said of him, 'so shall your offspring be.' Without weakening in his faith, he faced the fact that his body was as good as dead---since he was about a hundred years old---and that Sarah's womb was also dead. Yet he did not waver through unbelief regarding the promise of God, but was strengthened in his faith and gave glory to God, being fully persuaded that God had the power to do what he had promised. This is why it was credited to him as righteousness. The words 'it was credited to him' were written not for him alone, but also for us, to whom God will credit righteousness---for us who believe in him who raised Jesus our Lord from the dead. He was delivered over to death for our sins and was raised to life for our justification." (Romans 4:25) Every Easter Christians celebrate the resurrection of Jesus Christ from the dead. It is a celebration because it means death has been conquered.

Our sins have been paid in full through the death, burial and resurrection of Jesus Christ our Lord. In Romans 5:12 the Apostle Paul wrote that death entered the world through sin. He also wrote that death had been swallowed up in victory; it had lost its victory and sting because of the death and resurrection of our Lord Jesus Christ. (1 Corinthians 15:55)

The "he" that was to be born of a woman has come into the world. Christians celebrate that advent on Christmas. He was sent by the father to die for the sins of mankind so we could be holy as God is holy. Jesus made it possible for our sins to be forgiven and thus be made holy through Jesus Christ's death on the cross. The fact that those sins have been completely paid for is found in the resurrection. Jesus is no longer dead. The debt owed to God because of our sins has been completely paid for by Jesus Christ. The Bible says the result of that is "peace with God." (Romans 5:1) Have you ever been in a situation like a gathering where you were very uncomfortable because someone was there to whom you owed something, like a apology for wrongdoing or money you owed them? In the presence of God there is no longer a need to feel uncomfortable because of our guilt for deeds which we have done. God says he doesn't remember our sins against us anymore. He buried our sin in the deepest sea, to be forever removed and forgotten. (Micah 7:19) The Psalmist wrote, "For as high are the heavens above the earth, so great is his love for those who fear him; as far as the east is from the west, so far has he removed our transgressions from us." (Psalm 103:11-12) That means what Jesus said recorded for us in from John 3:16, "For God so loved the world that he gave his only begotten son, that whosoever believes on him, should not perish, but have everlasting life."

Questions:

1. What is it like knowing you have peace with God?

_____

_____

_____

2. From the account quoted above from Romans 4, what exactly did the people in the Old Testament have to do to be saved from the penalty of their sin?

_____

_____

_____

3. God said there would be "enmity" between the seed of woman and Satan's seed. Describe this "enmity" in history. Where do you observe this "enmity" now?

_____

_____

_____

4. Describe the uniqueness of Jesus from the genealogies of Matthew and Luke.

_____

_____

_____

5. What new insights did you glean from the statements Noah made to his sons?

_____

_____

_____

6. What was the curse on Canaan and how has it affected history?

    _____

    _____

    _____

7. How does legalism negatively influence a Christian's walk
    with the Lord Jesus Christ?

    _____

    _____

    _____

8. Can you identify the presence of legalism in your life? If
    yes, how are you attempting to eliminate it?

    _____

    _____

    _____

Chapter Six

B efore leaving the subject of the Flood, a few more things must be written. When I was in school, I had to study some of the writings of Neo-orthodox theologians like Emil Brunner. He emphasized that the Bible was about God's love to the exclusion of God's nature as one who is holy. He therefore concluded that the Noahic flood, an act of God's judgment, revealed a God who did not care about the value and worth of human life. He was forced to conclude this since he didn't understand God's holiness and therefore could not view the Flood as an expression of that holiness. Dr. Carl F. H. Henry in Volume 6 of his "God, Revelation and Authority", in a Chapter on the Holiness of God, would not support that conclusion from this Neo-orthodox theologian. He wrote, "The Bible insists upon man's created dignity no less than upon his depravity in sin; what's more, the God of the Bible offers man a means of divine rescue from ethical degradation and opportunity for moral renewal. The imprecatory Psalms are often deplored as subethical declarations of personal vindictiveness. But that verdict misreads their character. The Hebrews were divinely promised a land and those who would have destroyed the Israelites were regarded as the enemies of God (Psalm 139:21ff). What exactly the imprecatory Psalms exhibit is a zeal for righteousness."

This same zeal for righteousness is the product of God's holiness. The Bible portrays God as holy. For example, in Psalm 77:13 are these words penned, "Your way, O God, is holy." In Exodus 15:11 are recorded these words of Moses, "Who is like you, O Lord...majestic in holiness". And God himself spoke of his holiness recorded by the Prophet Hosea, "I am God, and not a man; the holy one in the midst of you." (Hosea 11:9) The Bible teaches that to think of God is to think of holiness. Holiness is his ruling attribute. This attribute explains the Flood. The thought of God's holiness dominated the thoughts of Isaiah about God. Isaiah, the prophet, wrote, "Holy, holy, holy is the Lord Almighty; the whole earth is full of his glory." Twenty eight times Isaiah refers to God as the "holy one". It is that holiness that the Bible puts on display from the very outset. There were consequences that God gave to mankind if he sinned. Those consequences are rooted in the divine nature of holiness. God is holy and therefore would not fellowship with mankind if they were sinful. God wants more than anything to be in fellowship with mankind so he warned them not to sin and thereby become unholy. Therefore the Bible is full of divine commandments and dire warnings against disobedience to the will of God. This is why the Bible reveals that Adam and Eve were driven out of the Garden of Eden. They had become unholy because of their sin. Lot and his family had to flee Sodom and Gomorrah because of God's punishment on the sin of those cities. Samson was given God's strength to kill the Philistines and bring their temple down upon them as judgment for their sin. The fact that God waives his right to judge mankind again by a flood (Genesis 8:21) does not in any way reveal a flaw in God's holy character. The Bible reveals a future judgment will occur on all mankind where mankind's behavior will be reviewed by God. The Father has appointed the Lord Jesus Christ to sit as judge during that review. (John 5:22-24)

After the destruction of the temple in Jerusalem by the Romans in 70 A.D., the Jews no longer referred to God by his holy name "Yahweh"; instead they used the expression "the Name" to refer to their holy God. Prior to that date, the Bible uses the word "holy" unapologetically to describe God. The Apostle John in 1 John 2:20 declared to believers, "But you have an anointing from the holy one and all of you know the truth." (The meaning of "the truth" can be gleaned from my book, "The Truth About The Lie" published by Zulon Press) The Apostle Peter when preaching at Pentecost in Acts 3:14 referred to Jesus as "the holy and righteous one". When Mary was told of her pregnancy by the angel, he said to her, "The Holy Spirit will come upon you, and the power of the Most High will overshadow you; therefore the child to be born will be called holy, the Son of God." (Luke 1:35) Karl Barth in his book, "Church Dogmatics", wrote that he thought Hebrews 10:26-31 was without parallel on the theme of God's holiness. That passage of Scripture states, "If we keep on sinning after we have received the knowledge of the truth, no sacrifice for sins is left, but only a fearful expectation of judgment and of raging fire that will consume the enemies of God. Anyone who rejected the law of Moses died without mercy on the testimony of two or three witnesses. How much more severely do you think a man deserves to be punished, who has trampled the Son of God under foot, who has treated as an unholy thing the blood of the covenant that sanctified him, and insulted the Spirit of grace? For we know him who said, 'It is mine to avenge, I will repay,' and again 'The Lord will judge his people.' It is a fearful thing to fall into the hands of the living God."

It is important to remember the author of the book of Hebrews had just written about the Law of God. (Hebrews 9:18-22) The Jews believed the Law was authored by God through Moses. It was therefore regarded as divinely inspired. Then the writer added, "When Moses had proclaimed every commandment to the people, he took the blood of calves, together with water, scarlet wool and branches of hyssop, and sprinkled the scroll and all the people. He said, 'This is the blood of the covenant which God has commanded you to keep.' In fact, the law requires that almost everything be cleansed with blood, and without the shedding of blood there is no forgiveness."

The seriousness of what the author of Hebrews is writing is understood from the fact that the New Covenant is greater than the old covenant given by Moses. It is greater since Jesus is greater than Moses (Hebrews 3:1ff) and his blood that ratifies it is greater than the blood of bulls and goats. (Hebrews 8:6; 9:23) There is, therefore, now a new covenant that God has made with mankind that also requires blood to be ratified. The blood that ratifies the New Covenant is the blood of Jesus Christ. Jesus verified this at the last supper that he had with his disciples. He said as he raised the cup, "Drink from it, all of you. This is my blood of the covenant, which is poured out for the many for the forgiveness of sins." (Matthew 26:27-28) Hebrews 9:12 declares Christ entered the Most Holy Place to offer his own blood to take away sins. This is the blood that was being "trampled under foot" and called meaningless by some. Therefore, when we take communion as directed by the Lord Jesus Christ, we are drinking a symbol of the blood that takes away our sins. When a Christian "confesses their sins" (1 John 1:9), the Bible assures the believer that God is faithful and will forgive the sins they have confessed. The Greek word translated "confess" comes from two Greek words which mean to name the sin. When we name the sin for which we want forgiveness, God forgives us. However, his forgiveness doesn't end there. 1 John 1:9 continues by stating "and cleanses us from all unrighteousness." The meaning is clear. The blood Jesus shed on the cross is the basis of his forgiveness. He cleanses us not only of the sins we confess, but also all the sins we do not remember or recall. He does this so we can be sinless, or, if you would, holy. In this condition we are obedient to what the Apostle Peter said about God when he said, "Be holy as I am holy." When we are holy, we are in the spiritual condition God planned for from the beginning of the world. One of the heavenly "blessings" God had in mind for us from the beginning of the world was that we be holy. Ephesians 1:2-3 says, "Blessed be the God and Father of our Lord Jesus Christ who has blessed us with every spiritual blessing in heavenly places, just as he chose us in him from the foundations of the world that we should be holy and blameless before him in love." When in this condition of holiness, God invites us to "present our bodies to him, a holy and living sacrifice..." (Romans 12:1-2) This is what we are to do to worship according to these same verses. The "therefore" is there in this verse because the Apostle Paul is drawing a conclusion from his arguments recorded in Romans 6-8.

In Romans 6:12 are these instructions from the Apostle Paul to every believer in Christ Jesus; "Do not let sin reign in your mortal body!" This admonition assumes that the Christian has a will and is able to exercise it in choices they are to make. First, the Christian is to recognize the existence of "sin" in their life. The word "sin" is in the singular tense and thus refers to the old nature (Adamic nature) that every person who is ever born has in them from birth. It appears in every person by virtue of the sin of Adam and Eve. Because of their sin, we have this sin nature in us. Even after we become a Christian, this nature continues to exist in us. When a person becomes a Christian they are justified through the work of Jesus Christ on the cross. Justification means the penalty of our sin is removed. However, remaining in every Christian who is justified still has the sin nature in them. The Bible describes the activity of the sinful nature as follows: "For the sin nature desires what is contrary to the Spirit, and the Spirit what is contrary to the sinful nature. They are in conflict with each other." (Galatians 5:17) The Apostle Paul in Romans 6:12 instructs the believer to choose between the Spirit and the sin nature as to which one will reign, ie. be in control, in their lives. Paul warns that if you choose the sin nature, sometimes referred to as the "flesh" in Scripture, you will end up succumbing to its evil desires. Galatians 5:19-21 illuminates what behavior types those evil desires could produce: "sexual immorality, impurity and debauchery, idolatry and witchcraft, hatred, discord, jealousy, fits of rage, selfish ambition, dissensions, factions and envy, drunkenness, orgies and the like."

Secondly, the Christian is directed by the Apostle Paul to "offer yourselves to God, as those who have been brought forth from death to life, and offer the parts of your body to him as instruments of righteousness." (Romans 6:13) Once the Christian does this, then they are filled with the Spirit. (Ephesians 5:18) Then, in that spiritual condition, they will manifest the fruits of the Holy Spirit which are "love, joy, peace, patience, goodness, kindness, faithfulness, gentleness and self control." (Galatians 5:22-23) The Apostle Paul goes on to say that these characteristics cannot be legislated by law, or manufactured from within us, but that they flow from the presence of God reigning in our lives.

Returning to the point the book of Hebrews makes about the blood of the new covenant, the kind of Spirit filled life just described is made possible through the blood of Christ who ratified the New Covenant. That covenant is described by the Apostle Paul in his second letter to the church at Corinth. He wrote to them and explained that God "made him competent as a minister of the new covenant---not of the letter but of the Spirit, for the letter kills, but the Spirit gives life." (2 Corinthians 3:6) The New Covenant in essence is God doing something for us, namely living the Christian life, which we cannot do for ourselves. Often times churches try to legislate what their parishioners are suppose to do and say. The Apostle Paul explains that doesn't work because of the nature of the flesh. In Romans 8:1ff, Paul makes the point that the sin nature is like a big stallion that has been put in a corral. The stallion sees the fence and jumps over it. It will not be contained by a corral. The corral here represents the attempts by some people to legislate good behavior. They are legalists attempting to contain and control their sinful nature by establishing laws. However, that will not work. Paul, using his own life's experiences said he didn't do the good he wanted to do and the things he didn't want to do, he did. In exasperation, he asked, "Who will rescue me from this body of death?" The answer to his question is then given, "Thanks be to God---through Jesus Christ our Lord." (Romans 7:24-25) And later he wrote, "For what the law was powerless to do in that it was weakened by the sinful nature, God did by sending his own Son in the likeness of sinful man to be a sin offering." Therefore we as Christians can choose to let the Spirit of God live the Christian life for us according to the New Covenant. Then we can be holy and righteous and move each day towards becoming more righteous as God works in our life. This is the meaning of 2 Corinthians 3:18 which describes that journey towards maturity when the Apostle Paul wrote, "And we, who with unveiled faces all reflect the Lord's glory, are being transformed into his likeness with ever-increasing glory, which comes from the Lord, who is the Spirit."

This last verse just quoted uses a couple of terms that need explaining. First, when the Apostle Paul referred to "unveiled faces", he was referring to what he had been written earlier about an event that had occurred in the life of Moses. (Exodus 34:29-35) Moses had gone up Mt. Sinai to meet with God and receive two tablets on which was written the Law. The Bible says that Moses returned from that meeting unaware that his face was radiant from being in the presence of God. "When Aaron and all the Israelites saw Moses, his face was radiant, and they were afraid to come near him. But Moses called to them, so Aaron and all the leaders of the community came back to him, and he spoke to them. Afterward all the Israelites came near him, and he gave them all the commandments the Lord had given him on Mount Sinai. When Moses finished speaking to them, he put a veil over his face. But whenever he entered the Lord's presence to speak with him, he removed the veil until he came out. And when he came out and told the Israelites what he had been commanded, they saw that his face was radiant. Then Moses would put the veil back over his face until he went in to speak with the Lord." Eventually, the radiance began to fade, but Moses kept putting the veil on so no one would notice. The veil had become the basis for his standing as leader of the Israelites. It became a substitute for the fact that God's word had established him a leader. As I wrote earlier in this book about the threat of legalism and that it establishes another basis for right standing before God and his people other than his word, so Moses is guilty of doing the same thing with the veil. When a Christian believes something they have done provides right standing before God, they "trample under foot" the blood of Jesus Christ that forgives sin and provides a right standing before God. The Bible says "By grace we are saved, and that not of ourselves, it is the gift of God, not of works, lest any man should boast." (Ephesians 2:8-9) That is why the Apostle Paul wrote "with unveiled face" in 2 Corinthians 3:18. In order to grow into maturity in our Christian lives, the Christian must come to God on the basis of Christ's work on the cross for us, and nothing else. There is nothing a Christian can offer God for the forgiveness of his sins and right standing (holiness) before him. Therefore, if you have a veil, take it off!

A second term needing explanation is the word "glory." Glory is the word that is used to describe the results of God's work. For example, Psalm 19:1 declares "The heavens declare the glory of God; the skies proclaim the work of his hands." Wherever God works, the results of that work give glory to him. Therefore, the phrase used in 2 Corinthians 3:18, "...all reflect the Lord's glory", is a statement that declares God is at work in us. The fantastic work he does in us gives him glory. The phrase "ever-increasing glory" means that God is at work in every area of our life. He works to make us a better God-centered father to our children. But that is not the end of his work. He is also working to make us a better God-centered wife or husband, if married. Again, his ever-increasing glory is discovered as he makes us a God-centered worker. His glory in the church is found among those believers allowing God to use their spiritual gifts to edify other believers. The list of areas in your life where God desires to glorify himself continues on and on. The Holy Spirit will prompt you as to what those areas are. For example, Revelation 3:20 declares that God "knocks on the door of our heart." The door upon which he knocks is the passageway into those areas where he is asking permission to work. God is the perfect gentleman in that he will only work in those areas in which he is given permission. As this process occurs, 2 Corinthians states that the Christian is "transformed into the likeness of God himself." Wherever God is allowed to work the Bible declares to be a work of reconstruction resulting in God's glory through grace. One of those special areas where he is at work is recorded in Ephesians 1:6 which states, "To the praise of his glorious grace he had made us accepted in the Beloved." God began his work to make you like himself by placing you in Christ Jesus. Jesus referenced the same thought when he said to his disciples, "On that day you will know that I am in the Father, you in me and I in you." The day to which Jesus is referring is the Day of Pentecost when the Holy Spirit was sent to baptize believers into Jesus Christ. This, among many others blessings, is what God has given to us. Ephesians 1:3 recorded how Paul began his letter to the church at Ephesus, "Blessed be the God and Father of our Lord Jesus Christ who has blessed us with every spiritual blessing in heavenly places." Part of that blessing is now to be able to "put off your old self, which is being corrupted by its deceitful desires to be made new in the attitude of our minds, and to put on the new self, created to be like God in true righteousness and holiness." (Ephesians 4:22-24)

It is important to add that when the Bible says God's plan for us is to like him, he doesn't mean in the sense that Satan wants to like God. Satan wants to be worshipped as a god. He does not want to be like God. His pride wouldn't let him settle for that. In contrast, God wants us to be like him as he shares with us his transitive attributes of love and holiness. His immutable attributes of omniscience, omnipotence and omnipresence belong to what it means to be God. These he does not share with us.

Questions:

1. Describe how the meaning of 2 Corinthians 3:18 has challenged your thinking about the Christian life.

_____

_____

_____

2. Read Ephesians 1:3-10. Describe some of the blessings listed there and what they mean to you.

_____

_____

_____

3. What areas in your life reflect the "glory" of God?

_____

_____

_____

4. What do you think of when you take Communion and drink the cup?

_____

_____

_____

5. What cannot the Old Covenant do?

_____

_____

_____

6. What condition must exist before we can see God? (Hebrews 12:14) Does 1 Peter 1:14-16 relate to this verse in the book of Hebrews? How?

_____

_____

_____

7. Jesus called the Pharisees a "brood of vipers" and "the blind leading the blind." What were the Pharisees teaching that Jesus found so offensive?

_____

_____

_____

8. Summarize this Chapter.

Chapter Seven

What has been happening in history and is happening now can be explained in part by understanding the direction where our future is headed. Satan, who is the god of this world, (2 Corinthians 4:4) has had a plan for this world since he left the Garden of Eden. That plan includes his strategy to remain god of this world. He has been sowing the seeds in history that will bring forth the fruit necessary to accomplish that goal. Satan knows that God also has a plan for the future of the world. He knows that for his own plan to be successful, he has to keep God's plan from succeeding. God's plan was revealed to Satan before he left the Garden of Eden. God said to Satan, "And I will put enmity between you and the woman, and between your seed and her seed, he will crush your head, and you will strike his heel." (Genesis 3:15) Satan didn't believe what God had told him. His thought pattern about what God had said was revealed in the Garden of Eden when he told Eve, contrary to what God had said, "You shall not surely die." (Genesis 3:4) One of the strategies of Satan to accomplish his goal is to hinder people from knowing the word of God. One way Satan does this is illustrated in the Book of Acts. Wherever the Apostle Paul traveled on his missionary journeys, resistance to the Gospel he preached materialized, either by the Jews who followed the Mosaic Law as prescribed in the Old Testament, or by people who were adherents of the false religions Satan had established throughout Asia Minor. An example of the latter was found in Ephesus recorded in Acts 19. Many people believed in Jesus Christ when Paul preached there in Ephesus. However, there was also resistance that originated in people there who worshipped Artemis. In fact, at one place where the Apostle Paul was preaching, the people chanted "Great is Artemis." They chanted this continually for two hours. A Silversmith there in Ephesus named Demetrius was upset because the Gospel would take business away from him. He realized if people no longer believed in Artemis, but instead worshipped God through Jesus Christ the Lord, they no longer would purchase the silver images of Artemis that he was making out of silver. Therefore he caused a rebellion to occur against Paul because of the Gospel he preached. That kind of resistance Satan has orchestrated wherever the Gospel has been preached down through the Centuries. Jesus had warned his disciples that the same hatred the world had towards him would also be directed towards them. These words of Jesus are recorded in John 15:18, "If the world hates you, keep in mind that it hated me first."

When Paul was in Jerusalem (Acts 22-23) he was arrested when some Jews from Asia Minor saw him in the temple. They lied to the people saying Paul had brought a Gentile into the temple. They stirred up the people so much that forty men took an oath not to eat until they had put Paul to death. A group of Roman soldiers had to transport Paul away from Jerusalem and took him to Caesarea. This is yet another illustration of the resistance Satan had organized to keep the Gospel from being heard.

Another example of the way Satan is combative towards the word of God is illustrated in the Book of Daniel. Daniel was a prophet of God's whose job as a prophet, was to tell God's people, Israel, what God wanted them to know. God would reveal his words to the prophets and they in turn would share it with his people. In this case, the prophet Daniel had been studying the revelations of an earlier prophet named Jeremiah. Jeremiah had spoken to the people of Israel, "Therefore the Lord Almighty says this: 'Because you have not listened to my words, I will summon all the peoples of the north and my servant Nebuchadnezzar king of Babylon,' declares the Lord, 'and I will bring them against this land and its inhabitants and against all the surrounding nations. I will completely destroy them and make them an object of horror and scorn, and an everlasting ruin. I will banish from them the sounds of joy and gladness, the voices of bride and bridegroom, the sound of millstones and the light of the lamp. This whole country will become a detestable wasteland, and these nations will serve the king of Babylon seventy years. But when the seventy years are completed..." (Jeremiah 25:8-12) The prophet Daniel wanted to know more about the seventy year prophecy, so he prayed to God to give him understanding of the prophecy. The angel Gabriel was dispatched by God to give him an answer to his prayer request. Gabriel said to Daniel, "I have now come to give you insight and understanding. As soon as you began to pray, an answer was given, which I have come to give to you, for you are highly esteemed. Therefore consider the message and understand the vision.

"Seventy 'sevens' are decreed for your people and your holy city to finish transgression, to put an end to sin, to atone for wickedness, to bring in everlasting righteousness, to seal up vision and prophecy and to anoint the most holy. Know and understand this: From the issuing of the decree to restore and rebuild Jerusalem until the Anointed One, the ruler, comes, there will be seven 'sevens' and sixty-two 'sevens'. It will be rebuilt with streets and a trench (walls), but in times of trouble. After the sixty-two 'sevens', the Anointed One will be cut off and will have nothing. The people of the ruler who will come will destroy the city and the sanctuary. The end will come like a flood: War will continue to the end, and desolations have been decreed. He will confirm a covenant with many for one 'seven.' In the middle of the 'sevens', he will put an end to the sacrifice and offering. And on a wing of the temple, he will set up an abomination that causes desolation, until the end that is decreed is poured out on him." (Daniel 9:24-27) In fulfillment of this prophecy, king Artaxerxes, king of the Medes and Persians, granted Nehemiah permission to return to Jerusalem from Susa to rebuild the city and the walls. (Nehemiah 2:8) The Medes and Persians had conquered Babylon and inherited the Jewish people whom the Babylonians had taken them into captivity when they conquered Israel. Archaeologists have discovered a stele with the date recorded on it of that edict of Artaxerxes. It was given on March 15, 445 B.C. according to a book entitled, "The Coming Prince", authored by Sir Robert Anderson. The prophecy stated that there would be 69 weeks of years or 69x7 years. The total amount of years was 483 years. That amount of time would elapse from the time permission was given to Nehemiah to return to Jerusalem until the Anointed One would appear in Jerusalem. We know this was the city to which the Messiah would return based on the fact that this prophecy pertained to Israel and Jerusalem. (Daniel 9:24) In the Jewish calendar there were 360 days. This prophecy there-fore was predicting the Messiah, the Anointed One, would arrive in Jerusalem 173,880 days after king Artaxerxes gave permission for Nehemiah to return to Jerusalem. Using the Roman calendar which has 365 days in a year, Jesus arrived in Jerusalem on April 6th, 32 A.D. If you add 445 and 32, the total number of years is 477. However, we need to subtract one year from that total since there is just one year between 1 B.C. and 1 A.D. If you then mul-tiply 476x365, the total is 173,740. If you then add 116 years for leap years and 24 for the days between April 6 and March 15, the total is 173,880. God's time clock began ticking on March 15, 445 B.C. If one used the Jewish calendar with 360 days, by multiplying 360x476 one discovers that the answer is also 173,880 days. Both the Jewish and Roman calendars predicted the same day Jesus Christ, the Messiah, would enter Jerusalem. Therefore the people, the Scribes, the Pharisees and teachers of the Law should have been counting down and should have expected the Messiah 173,880 days after the date of March 15th, 445 B.C. When Jesus rode into Jerusalem on what is now called Palm Sunday, they should have recognized him as their Messiah. He rode into Jerusalem on the exact day that the prophet Daniel prophesied. Jesus even referred to this fact in his words recorded in Luke 19:44, "They will dash you to the ground, you and the children within your walls. They will not leave one stone on another, because you did not recognize the time of God's visitation to you." Satan had blinded the Spiritual leadership of Israel to the time of God's visitation by having them focus on the mundane things related to the temple. They were selling the different sacrifices the people were to give to the priests who would in turn offer them as sacrifices for their sins. The exorbitant prices for these sacrifices made this a lucrative business for the priests and Pharisees. They were not doing their jobs as good shepherds of God's people. God had told Israel when he would be coming, but they were unaware of it because they were not students of the Bible. Satan had redirected their focus away from the Bible so they were ignorant of it.

Another example of Satan's work of hindering the knowledge of God and his work is recorded also in the book of Daniel. Daniel had had another angel visit him as recorded in Daniel 10. That angel told Daniel "you are highly esteemed. Consider carefully the words I am about to speak to you, and stand up, for I have now been sent to you...Do not be afraid, Daniel. Since the first day you set your mind to gain understanding and to humble yourself before your God, your words were heard and I have come in response to them. But the prince of the Persian kingdom resisted me twenty-one days. Then Michael, one of the chief princes, came to help me, because I was detained there with the prince of Persia." (Daniel 10:10-13) These Chapters in the Book of Daniel explain God's desire to give us his word. They also explain that Satan wants to keep that from happening. Proverbs 29:18 explains why knowing the Bible is so important. That verse states that "Without a vision, the people perish." The word "vision" is better translated "revelation". This verse is written as poetry using parallelism to communicate the meaning. The word "law" is in line two and compliments the word "vision". God's law was revealed through the prophet Moses. All the prophets in the Old Testament were chosen by God to write and proclaim to the people what God had said to them. Without that revelation, Proverbs 29:18 reports that the people "perish". Literally this word means they act in an unrestricted fashion. One commentary said the word means to "let their hair down." Another picture explaining the word "perish" would be of a blind person wandering around an apartment not knowing where the furniture was so he would stumble when he bumped into it. "Perishing meant that their actions reflected that there was no law restraining their behavior. Therefore, "anything goes", or anarchy occurs, when God's word is absent. A Biblical illustration of that kind of behavior was found in the cities of Sodom and Gomorrah. God destroyed those cities because of the immorality and homosexual activity practiced in those cities.

Another illustration of people acting without restraint, were the people in Portland, Oregon and Minneapolis, Minnesota, during the summer of 2020. There were rioters who burnt buildings and killed small business owners trying to protect their own stores. The police, who could have restrained that behavior, had been removed from doing their duties. Even now, in cities where the police force has been reduced in number, there is a growing number of homicides, burglaries and rapes. The purpose of a police force is to act in the same capacity as the revelation of God. They are to thwart violence as the word of God does when it is allowed to work in individual lives. Romans 12:1ff teaches this same truth. Lives are changed as people's thinking is changed by responding obediently to God's word. The result of that changed thinking is changes in behavior. In Romans 12:2 God instructs us "not to be conformed to this world, but to be transformed by the renewing of your mind, so that you know what the will of God is." In 1 Corinthians 6:9-11 the Apostle Paul wrote, "Do you not know that the wicked will not inherit the kingdom of God? Do not be deceived: Neither the sexually immoral nor idolaters nor adulterers nor male prostitutes nor homosexual offenders nor thieves nor the greedy nor the slanderers nor drunkards nor swindles will inherit the kingdom of God. And that is what some of you were. But you were washed, you were sanctified and you were justified in the name of the Lord Jesus Christ and by the Spirit of our God." Without God's revelation found in the Bible, people would not know about the power of God to change their lives through the work of Jesus Christ on the cross. Satan wants people to remain slaves to their sinful desires that originate in the flesh. Therefore he does all he can to hide the word of God from mankind. Then he can introduce them to the false religions he has designed to hide them from the truth found in the Bible. He does not want people to know about Jesus Christ and his work on the cross to save them from their sin.

Satan is also at work behind the scenes today in those countries which persecute Christians for their faith in Jesus Christ. Through persecutions, Satan tries to create a fear of Christianity and thus dissuade people from investigating the claims of Jesus Christ that could change their lives and eternal destinies. Satan has also deceived many countries in the world to be antagonistic towards the church. The leaders in those countries want to retain the power to govern their countries. They do not want God interfering with their positions of authority. Therefore they oppress those whose authority is God. This information doesn't receive much attention from the liberal press that exists in our country. However, the oppression exists just the same. In some countries just going into a church can result in prison time. Just by wearing a cross can lead to the same action against that person.

In China, that dictatorship discriminates against Christians by invading homes used for Bible studies and the worship of God. The Christians are thrown into prison and jails much like the adherents of Islam are. One Christian recently released from jail in China had spent 10 months there and was subjected to physical assaults by the guards. He reported that women are raped and if they become pregnant, abortions are performed. This kind of behavior describes nations that have been deceived by the Devil and his fallen angels. Jesus described this kind of behavior while describing events that would occur towards the end of the church age. In Matthew 24:9-12 these words of Jesus are recorded, "Then you will be handed over to be persecuted and put to death, and you will be hated by all nations because of me. At that time many will turn away from the faith and will betray and hate one another, and many false prophets will appear and deceive many people. Because of the increase of wickedness the love of most will grow cold, but he who stands firm to the end will be saved."

There are verses in Revelation 19-20 that describe the activity of Satan and his angels as "deceivers" that will lead nations to even fight against Jesus Christ himself. Those deceptions have occurred and are occurring now amongst the nations of the world. Every nation hostile to the Gospel and to Christian churches and the Gospel they preach are victims of that deception. The Apostle Paul instructed Christians to be aware of this and then to stand against the activity of Satan and his fallen angels. Recorded in Ephesians 6:10 and following are these words: "Finally, be strong in the Lord and in the power of his might. Put on the full armor of God so that you can take your stand against the devil's schemes. For our struggle is not against flesh and blood, but against the rulers, against the authorities, against the powers of this dark world and against the spiritual forces of evil in the heavenly realm. Therefore, put on the full armor of God, so that when the day of evil comes, you may be able to stand your ground, and after you have done everything, to stand. Stand firm then, with the belt of truth buckled around your waist, with the breastplate of righteousness in place, and with your feet shod with the gospel of peace. In addition to all this, take up the shield of faith, with which you can extinguish all the flaming arrows of the evil one. Take the helmet of Salvation and the sword of the Spirit, which is the word of God. And pray in the Spirit on all occasions with all kinds of prayers and requests. With this in mind, be alert and keep on praying for all the saints." The "day of evil", (Ephesians 6:13) referenced in these instructions, is to warn of a future day when "no man can work." Jesus called that day "night." (John 9:4) In the context of that statement, Jesus calls himself the light of the world. There is coming a time when to speak of Jesus and the light he brings to the world through the Gospel will be accompanied by a death sentence. That is why In the Book of Revelation 14:1ff, the "one hundred forty-four thousand witnesses" are given a special mark that will protect them from death. Without that protection these Jewish witnesses would be killed for preaching the good news of the Gospel. These 144,000 are the Jewish youth who heard the "two witnesses" mentioned in Revelation 11:13. They are the ones who survive the earthquake when the two witnesses were taken into heaven. The text says that "they gave glory to the God of heaven." (Revelation 11:13) That is an Old Testament idiom meaning that they placed faith in Jesus Christ as their Lord and Savior, the God of whom these two witnesses will proclaim themselves to be adherents. These one hundred forty-four thousand Jewish youths, 12,000 from each of the twelve tribes of Israel, (Revelation 7:4) will become Christians and they will proclaim to a world, hostile to the Gospel, who had just killed the two witnesses and rejoiced at their demise (Revelation 11:10), the same message for which those two witnesses will be killed. Their message is recorded in Revelation 14:7, "Fear God and give him glory, because the hour of his judgment has come.

Worship him who made the heavens and the earth, the sea and the springs of water." The Bible teaches that these 144,000 will proclaim the Gospel to the whole world. Their proclamation fulfills the prophecy of Jesus recorded in Matthew 24:14, "And the gospel of the kingdom will be proclaimed in the whole world as a testimony to all the nations, then the end will come."

Jesus spoke of a time yet to come when there would be great hostility towards Christians and Jews, resulting in the death of most of them. He identified that time as occurring immediately after the time the Antichrist will abolish temple sacrifice in Jerusalem. Matthew 24:15-22 recorded those words of Jesus, "So when you see the Abomination of Desolation, spoken of through the prophet Daniel---let the reader understand---then let those who are in Judea flee to the mountains. Let no one on the roof of his house go down to take anything out of his house. Let no one in the field go back to get his cloak. How dreadful it will be in those days for a pregnant woman and nursing mothers! Pray that your flight will not take place in winter or on the Sabbath. For there will be great distress, unequaled from the beginning of the world until now---never to be equaled again. If those days had not been cut short, no one would survive, but for the sake of the elect those days will be shortened." The reason for the warning of what happens in winter is this: flash floods occur. In Israel the roads go down into the valleys and then follow the terrain up the other side of the valley. There are few bridges and individuals in the valley would be swept away in a flash flood. These types of floods, for example, are very familiar to people in Colorado living on the eastern slope of the Rocky Mountains. When torrential rains come in the spring or summer, many people have died in flash floods. Some years ago some women returning from a weekend retreat with Campus Crusade for Christ were killed by a flash flood that gushed out of the Rocky Mountains.

Jesus words are directed to the Jewish community who were gathered in Jerusalem at the time of this discourse. However, those words are to be understood as pertaining to a future time for the Jewish community living in Jerusalem when temple sacrifice is abolished. That sacrificial system was instituted by God and practiced throughout the Old Testament history of the Jews. Once the temple is rebuilt in Jerusalem those sacrifices at the temple will resume again. That is the time Jesus is referring to when he speaks of the cessation of the sacrifices at the temple in Jerusalem. Satan wants to stop those practices designed to worship the God of Israel. Therefore he will indwell the Anti-Christ and use him to accomplish his will. After this event foretold by the prophet Daniel occurs, the Jewish population living in Israel is told to flee Judea by Jesus. The reason for this warning is that Satan wants to remain god of this world. He can achieve this goal by killing every Jewish person alive. The reason this is of extreme importance to understand is because Jesus said he would not return to earth as the Jewish Messiah until the Jews called him back. Read what Jesus said as recorded in Matthew 23:37-39: "O Jerusalem, Jerusalem, you who kill the prophets and stone those sent to you, how often I have longed to gather your children together, as a hen gathers her chicks together under her wings, but you were not willing. Look, you house is left to you desolate. For I tell you, you will not see me again until you say, "Blessed is he who comes in the name of the Lord.""

This phrase "Blessed is he who comes in the name of the Lord" is found in a Messianic Psalm in Psalm 118:21-27, "I will give you thanks, for you answered me; you have become my salvation. The stone the builders rejected has become the capstone; the Lord has done this, and it is marvelous in our eyes. This is the day the Lord has made; let us rejoice and be glad in it. O Lord, save us; O Lord, grant us success. Blessed is he who comes in the name of the Lord. From the house of the Lord we bless you. The Lord is God and has made his light shine upon us. With boughs in hand, join in the festal procession up to the horns of the altar." Derek Kidner in his book on the Psalms says that "the day which the Lord has made" is probably a reference to one of the annual feasts, either Passover, or Pentecost or Tabernacles. In this case it is Passover. It was God who appointed the feasts to be observed by Israel. (Leviticus 23) The "festal procession" is a celebration. Therefore, it is not a coincidence that the procession leading into Jerusalem was a celebration where the people with Palm branches were acknowledging Jesus as their Messiah. The people didn't realize it yet, but they were not only welcoming their Messiah, but also their Passover Lamb. (1 Corinthians 5:7) At this celebration of Passover, the Jews recited to Jesus entering Jerusalem on Palm Sunday, "Blessed is he who comes in the name of the Lord." In so doing they were welcoming their God. This procession led ultimately to the "horns of the altar" in the temple, which in this case was a procession eventually leading to the cross upon which Jesus would die and shed his blood. "The stone which the builders rejected" in this Psalm (Psalm 118:22) indicates that there would be resistance to the ministry of the Messiah. The "builders" therefore is a reference to the leadership in Israel at the time of Christ. This leadership rejected Jesus. The "builders" are the Pharisees that ruled in the Spiritual affairs of the people of Israel. When Jesus did miracles like causing a deaf and dumb person to hear and speak, the people said Jesus must be the Messiah, since the Messiah would be able to do that miracle. On the other hand, the Pharisees recognized what the possibilities were if the people accepted Jesus and rejected them. Therefore, the Pharisees said Jesus had done this miracle by the power of the Devil. They also rejected Jesus and plotted his death because they were afraid of losing their leadership positions. They said to one another, "If we let him go on like this, everyone will believe in him, and then the Romans will come and take away both our place and our nation...from that day on they plotted to take his life." (John 11:48, 53)

Questions:

1. How has your understanding of Psalm 118 changed your way of thinking about Palm Sunday?

_____

_____

_____

2. Read again Daniel 9:24-27. What is the abomination that makes desolate?

_____

_____

_____

3. Why should the people have known "the time of their visitation?"

_____

_____

_____

4. The "day of evil" is descriptive of what?

_____

_____

_____

5. Has this Chapter helped clear up some of your thinking about the 144,000? How?

_____

_____

_____

6. What do some of the cults teach about the 144,000?

_____

_____

_____

7. Since Jesus came into Jerusalem on the exact day foretold by the prophet Daniel, what about Christ's return of which you are now sure? Explain.

_____

_____

_____

8. How has your prayer life changed from reading this Chapter?

_____

_____

_____

9. One of the key passages for understanding prophecy is Matthew 23:37-39. Why?

_____

_____

_____

10. How does Matthew 23:37-39 assist in explaining anti-Semitism?

_____

_____

_____

Chapter Eight

The theme this book has been developing is that the god of this world, Satan, has a plan to forever retain that position and title. At the same time, he also knows the God who created this world has a plan to take this position away from him. This world and all that is in it was created by Jesus Christ. By virtue of that fact it belongs to him. Colossians 1:15-17 teaches us that Jesus "is the image of the invisible God, the firstborn over all creation. For by him all things were created: things in heaven and on earth, visible and invisible, whether thrones or powers or rulers and authorities, all things were created by him and for him." The phrase "for him" teaches us that ownership of this world belongs to Jesus Christ. He has the pink slip, if you would. Therefore he has a right to attempt to take it back from Satan who deceitfully stole it from him. That plan to take it back God shared with Satan face to face in the Garden of Eden when he said, "And I will put enmity between you and the woman, and between your offspring and hers; he will crush your head and you will strike his heel." (Genesis 3:15) The "he" that is referred to in this Scripture is the Lord Jesus Christ. He was born of a woman, Mary, as this Scripture predicted. That prediction is recorded in Isaiah 7:14, "Therefore the Lord himself will give you a sign. The virgin shall be with child and will give birth to a son, and will call him Immanuel." Previous to this promise of the virgin birth of the Messiah, "God with us" (The meaning of Immanuel) The context for this promise was that Israel was about to be invaded. God told King Ahaz not to fret or worry about the pending danger since he would protect Israel. God told Ahaz the king to ask God for a sign that he would keep his promise. Ahaz refused so God said then he would give him a sign. That sign was the virgin birth of Jesus Christ.

Once he was born, Satan tried to destroy the child that would take away his position as god of this earth. He did this by using the Magi who had come to Bethlehem to worship the Messiah. They informed King Herod that a rival to his throne had been born and that they had come to worship him. (Matthew 2:1-12) By consulting the Chief Priests and teachers of the Law, Herod learned where the Messiah was to be born. They discovered in the prophecy of Micah that he would be born in Bethlehem. (Micah 5:2) King Herod had learned from the Magi the approximate time the star had appeared announcing the birth so that later he could kill the child. After the Magi left, King Herod sent out a decree to have all the male children two years old and younger killed. (Matthew 2:16-18) Again Satan's strategy to retain his position as god was revealed. Jesus, being the first-born son of Mary and the adopted son of Joseph, was the only one who could fulfill the Scriptures and the promise given to David that the Messiah would be born of his lineage. If Jesus had been killed, the Messiah would have been killed and Salvation through him would no longer be possible. However, God being much more intelligent than Satan, being able to see the beginning of history and its end, warned Joseph in a dream to take Mary and their son, Jesus, and flee to Egypt where they would be safe. (Matthew 2:13) Once Herod died, God informed Joseph it was safe to return to Judea, namely to Nazareth. Though Satan's plan failed to destroy the Messiah and thus retain his position as god of this world, he had another plan ready to be initiated.

After Jesus was baptized, he went into the wilderness prior to starting his ministry. While there, Satan tempted him. Because he had not eaten the 40 days while he was there, Satan tempted him to turn stones into bread. Jesus' response was "It is written: Man shall not live on bread alone, but on every word that comes from the mouth of God." (Matthew 4:4) Then Satan tempted Jesus to throw himself off the highest point of the temple in Jerusalem to see if the Scriptures were true that God's angels would protect him. Jesus responded, "It is written, do not put the Lord your God to the test." (Matthew 4:7) Then he offered Jesus the position of a god working under his authority. Satan said that in that position he would have control of everything in the world. All he had to do was bow down and worship Satan as the god of this world. Imagine by worshipping that Jesus would exalt the character of Satan. Imagine then a world where lying, killing, rape and anarchy in general were allowed without any kind of restraint. Jesus was offered a position in Satan's government as god and in so doing, could evade the pain, rejection, and death by suffocation on a cross. Jesus responded with these words, "Away from me Satan, for it is written: 'Worship the Lord your God and serve him only.'" (Matthew 4:10)

Satan's plan failed but he still had another one ready to be initiated. That plan is understood from the Gospel accounts where they describe the arrest, trials and crucifixion of Jesus, the Messiah. When Jesus said on the cross, "It is finished", (John 19:30) God's plan was completed while Satan's was again thwarted. Then on the third day he arose from the dead. The Apostle Paul therefore wrote, "He was delivered over to death for our sins and was raised to life for our justification." (Romans 4:25) "Justification" refers to being in the condition of being blameless before God, as if the sinner had never sinned. When Justified by God, it is just as if you and I had never sinned! This spiritual condition exists once we believe in Jesus Christ as Savior and Lord. It is as if Satan brings us into the courtroom of God to condemn us of sin. Then God the judge looks at his ledger and responds, "What sin? I see no sin recorded against them in my record book. This person is free to go, being blameless before me." Jesus saved us from the penalty of our sin. By his resurrection, Jesus conquered the "wages of sin", death. (Romans 3:23) That truth prompted the Apostle Paul to write to the Church at Corinth, "Where, O death is your victory? Where, O death is your sting. The sting of death is sin, and the power of sin is the law. But thanks be to God! He gives us the victory through our Lord Jesus Christ." (1 Corinthians 15:55-57) To the church at Colossae, the Apostle Paul put it this way, "When you were dead in your sins and in the uncircumcision of your sinful nature, God made you alive with Christ. He forgave all your sins, having canceled the written code, with its regulations, that was against us and stood in opposition to us, he took it away having nailed it to the cross. And having disarmed the powers and authorities, he made a public spectacle of them, triumphing over them at the cross." (Colossians 2:13-15) This strategy of Satan failed along with his original plan to kill the Messiah when he was a baby. Now Satan has failed yet again to stop God's plan from taking effect. Satan "bruised his heel." (Genesis 3:15) That occurred when Jesus was put to death on the cross. However, in the process of doing that God "crushed the head" of the serpent, Satan. He did so through his resurrection. Jesus is alive!

Satan's strategies, to date, have not been that successful. However, he is not going to give up trying to retain his position as god of the world. For him to fail would mean suffering in the Lake of Fire forever. Therefore we can imagine how committed he is remaining god of this world. Though his attempts in the past have failed, he has a future plan already in place and he is working now to put the pieces of that plan into place to make it successful. Remember God's promise to Abraham that the world would be blessed through him. Remember also that that promise involved King David and one of his offspring, the Messiah, sitting on his throne and reigning forever. Therefore, understand Satan's strategy relative to God's promises to those individuals. Those men were Jews and therefore it is through the Jewish race that God's plan will be fulfilled. That is why Jesus elevated the Jews over the Gentiles with sayings like "to the Jews, first, and then the Gentiles," and "I was sent only to the lost sheep of Israel." (Matthew 15:24) Even at the Temple in Jerusalem, only Jews could go inside a particular area. Though there was a place for Gentiles to worship God at the temple in Jerusalem, it was outside of where the Jews went to worship. The Jewish people are "the apple of God's eye", for it is through them that he has worked his plan to save the world from its sin. He chose them to be his people and He would be their God. God said this to them recorded in Leviticus 11:44, "I am the Lord your God; consecrate yourselves and be holy because I am holy." Moses described this relationship when he wrote, "The Lord your God has chosen you out of all the peoples on the face of the earth to be his people, his treasured possession. The Lord did not set his affection upon you and choose you because you were more numerous than other peoples, for you were the fewest of all peoples. But it was because the Lord loved you and kept the oath that he swore to your forefathers that he brought you out with a mighty hand and redeemed you from the land of slavery, from the power of Pharaoh, king of Egypt. Know, therefore, that the Lord your God is God; he is the faithful God, keeping his covenant of love to a thousand generations of those who love him and keep his commandments." (Deuteronomy 7:7-9)

As his chosen people, God has given them an extremely important role to fulfill at the end of history. Gabriel announced that future role to Daniel. That role is recorded in Daniel 9:20-24, "While I was speaking and praying, confessing my sin and the sins of my people Israel and making my request to the Lord my God for his holy hill---While I was still in prayer, Gabriel, the man I had seen in an earlier vision, came to me in swift flight about the time of the evening sacrifice. He instructed me and said to me, 'Daniel, I have now come to give you insight and understanding. As soon as you began to pray, an answer was given, which I have come to tell you, for you are highly esteemed. Therefore consider the message and understand the vision: Seventy 'sevens' are decreed for your people and your holy city to finish transgression, to put an end to sin, to atone for wickedness, to bring in everlasting righteousness, to seal up vision and prophecy, and to anoint the most holy.'"

This information was given to Daniel and what it means became the focus of the book of Daniel. However, it is extremely important to note that what God had appointed the Jewish people to do, they were to accomplish during the Seventy weeks of years. The first of six job descriptions is to "restrain transgression". The verb translated "restrain" means to close, shut or restrain. It is written in the Hebrew Piel verb tense which indicates intensity. Therefore the phrase could read "to restrain firmly." The word translated "transgression", according to the Tyndale Old Testament Commentaries, is describing the "idea of rebellion and self-assertion, and this is describing sin in general and in its many forms." The Bible teaches that the "old nature" in man is the source of their rebellion against God. The Bible further teaches in Romans 6-8 that God destroyed the power of the old nature (flesh or sin in the singular) through Jesus Christ's death on the cross. Now the believer can say "no" to the flesh's attempt to manifest itself in selfish desires. Romans 6:6-7 teaches this when it says, "For we know that our old self was crucified with him so that the body of sin might be done away with, that we should no longer be slaves to sin---because anyone who has died has been freed from sin." The Apostle Paul continues Romans 6 with this application in verses 12-13, "Therefore, do not let sin reign in your mortal body so that you obey its evil desires. Do not offer the parts of your body to sin as instruments of wickedness, but rather offer yourselves to God, as those who have been brought forth from death to life, and offer the parts of your body to him as instruments of righteousness. For sin shall not be your master, because you are not under law, but under grace." God "restrained transgression firmly" according to Daniel 9:26 when the Messiah was killed. After his death, on the third day he arose from the grave. He is no longer dead, but alive and gives us the power of his resurrection for a completely new way of living. (Philippians 3) Ephesians 3:20-21 puts it this way, "Now to him who is able to do immeasurably more than all we can ask or think, according to his power which is at work within us, to him be glory in the church and in Christ Jesus throughout all generations, forever and ever! Amen." Through the work of Jesus Christ alluded to in Daniel 9:25-26, The Jewish people accomplished this first of six assignments given to them by God.

The next job description for the Jewish nation is "to put an end to sin." This statement is parallel to the previous one in meaning. The word for "sin" is used in the Old Testament to describe all wrong. It means literally to miss the mark. It is describing an archer raising his bow and shooting an arrow at the bulls-eye on the target. Not only does this word indicate the arrow missed the bulls-eye, but it missed the target altogether. There will be an end to sin when the Christian receives his resurrection body. 1 Corinthians 15 describes our earthly body as mortal. But at the resurrection, it will be raised immortal. The Jews accomplished this through the work of Christ on the cross.

The third part of the job description for the Jewish people is "to atone for wickedness." Leon Wood in his <u>Commentary on Daniel</u> wrote that this last statement explains how the first two would be accomplished. And of course we know that it is only by a personal receiving the gift of grace that Salvation occurs, and holiness is then used to describe that person's life. Atonement means literally "that God and the person of faith are at one." They are both holy. There is therefore an end to sin in that person's life. "Mr. Wood goes on to write, "Since Gabriel was speaking primarily in reference to the Jews, rather than the Gentiles, this fact requires the interpretation to include also Christ's Second Coming, because only then does Israel as a nation turn to Christ." Zechariah 13-14 describes Israel's repentance during the "last days." Interestingly, these Scriptures predict only about one-third of the nation will repent to call and welcome back their Messiah. (Zachariah 13:8-9)

A better understanding of the meaning of Atonement is gleaned from a study of Leviticus 16. That portion of Scripture describes the festivities surrounding the Day of Atonement, called in Hebrew Yom Kippur. The celebration was to rejoice in the fact that God loved his people and wanted to be "One" with them. It was a remembrance of a time when God met and walked with Adam and Eve in the Garden of Eden. This picture of God's fellowship with man and his desire to be with mankind was the meaning behind the ceremonies conducted on the Day of Atonement. It was the same picture Jesus painted when he told the story of the Prodigal Son. (Luke 15:11ff) However, the advent of sin destroyed that fellowship God had with Adam and Eve and subsequently with all mankind. God's plan to take away that sin was what the celebration on the Day of Atonement was all about.

The Day of Atonement originated with God in the same way God was in Christ reconciling the world to God. (2 Corinthians 5:19) The ceremony on the Day of Atonement began when two goats were brought before the High Priest. Then the High Priest would cast lots over the two goats. One lot was for the goat upon which the sins of the people would be placed. The High Priest would put his hands on that goat and confess the sins of Israel upon it. The other lot fell on the second goat called Azazel. The High Priest would then go into the Holy of Holies and offer the first goat on the altar to cover the sins of the people. Then the second goat, Azazel, would be led out of the camp and taken into the wilderness and left there. As the goat was taken out from among the people, they would throw rocks and hurl all kinds of insults at the goat. These actions showed the contempt the people had for their sins. The symbolism was clear. God takes our sins away and removes them "as far as the East is from the West." (Psalm 103:12) In the Book of Micah, God says they "are buried in the deepest sea" (Micah 7) and posts a sign saying "no fishing allowed." The International Standard Bible Encyclopedia interprets Hebrews 9:23-24 in light of the Day of Atonement, "Christ himself entered the holy place, which was not made with hands, namely heaven itself, and has now appeared before God, by once and for all giving himself as a sacrifice for the removal of sin."

The first of the three positive items the Jews are to do is "to bring in everlasting righteousness." The verb translated "to bring in" occurs in the Hiphil tense and means to "cause to come in". The Jewish people will cause the Messiah to return by calling him back and inviting him to be their Messiah. Remember Jesus said he would not return to earth as the Messiah until the Jews called him back. (Matthew 23:37-39) The actual words they use to call him back are recorded in the Old Testament. Remember the setting when these words will be spoken. They are spoken during the period of time known as Jacob's Trouble. They will be spoken during a time that Jesus described in Matthew 24:21-22, "For then there will be great distress, unequaled from the beginning of the world until now. If those days had not been cut short no one would survive, but for the sake of the elect, those days will be shortened." Read the words the Jews use to call back their Messiah, "Hear us, O Shepherd of Israel, you who lead Jacob like a flock; you who sit enthroned between the cherubim, shine forth. Before Ephraim, Benjamin and Manasseh, awaken your might; come and save us. Restore us, O God; make your face shine upon us, that we may be saved...Return to us, O God Almighty! Look down from heaven and see! Watch over this vine, the root your right hand has planted, the son you have raised up for yourself. Your vine is cut down, it is burned with fire; at your rebuke your people perish. Let your hand rest on the man at your right hand, the son of man you have raised up for yourself. Then we will not turn away from you; revive us and we will call on your name. Restore us, O Lord God Almighty. Make your face shine upon us that we may be saved." (Psalm 80) A similar calling back of Jesus as the Jewish Messiah is recorded in Hosea 6:1-3, "Come, let us return to the Lord. He has torn us to pieces but he will heal us; he has injured us, but he will bind up our wounds. After two days he will revive us; on the third day he will restore us that we may live in his presence. Let us acknowledge the Lord; let us press on to acknowledge him. As surely as the sun rises, he will appear. He will come to us like the winter rains, like the spring rains that water the earth." With these words, the Jewish people will call back their Messiah, Jesus Christ, who is the King of Kings and Lord of Lords.

"Everlasting" is needed here since Israel in the past had been on a rollercoaster. They would go through periods of repentance after God disciplined them for some sin, and then later would again have to be disciplined for another sin. Everlasting means the rollercoaster is over. Their righteousness would be permanent. The same is true for the Christian. There are times due to Christ's resurrection that Christians give their lives to God as instruments of righteousness (Romans 6:13). There is no sin in their life. However, that condition can change when we yield to temptation and live for the flesh. To return to a sanctified life, the Christian has to repent and then confess their sin. (1 John 1:9) Then God forgives us and cleanses us from all unrighteousness. Then we are holy and righteous. To "bring in an everlasting righteousness" involves eliminating sin as a possible choice for the believer. This occurs at two events in time. The first is the Rapture of the church. (1 Thessalonians 4:13-17) When this event occurs, every believer in Jesus Christ on earth will be caught up to heaven, both the living and the dead. Then at some point, we will receive our resurrection bodies. They will have no "sin nature" and we will worship our Lord and Savior through our love and obedience to him. Clothed in righteousness will allow us to enter the Marriage Supper of the Lamb in heaven. In a parable, Jesus taught that no one will be allow into that event without proper clothing, namely the righteousness of God. (Revelation 19:9; Matthew 22:11) After the Rapture the righteousness given by God to the believer will be permanent. However, after the Rapture, there will be left here on earth those that are not believers. After the 144,000 are sealed and commissioned, (Revelation 14) they will go out to the world evangelizing the world and preaching the Gospel. At this time the prophecy of Jesus will be fulfilled, "And this gospel of the kingdom will be preached in the whole world as a testimony to all nations, then the end shall come." (Matthew 24:14) The result of that preaching will be a great spiritual harvest of new believers in Jesus Christ. Given the context of their new faith in Jesus Christ, they will be the object of anger within the world government called the beast and the anti-Christ. Christians will be killed for their faith. Revelation 20:4, "And I saw the souls of those who had been beheaded because of their testimony for Jesus and because of the word of God."

Then Jesus will return "To seal up vision." This refers to finishing the purpose of revelation which had been given by the prophets. Dr. Leon Wood in his commentary on Daniel wrote, "The time in mind can only be the final days of the world when Christ comes in power. Many prophecies still remain unfulfilled and require that such a day occur. Much prophecy pertaining to the last days are found in the Old and New Testament which were not fulfilled at Christ's first coming. It awaits the day yet future." "To anoint a holy of holies" is the final instruction revealed to Daniel explaining the role of the Jews in history. "To anoint" means to consecrate for religious service. The phrase "Holy of holies" is a reference to the temple since the definite article in not used. When Jesus Christ returns the second time, there will be a temple in Jerusalem consecrated for his ministry there as the King of Kings and Lord of Lords. However, until Jesus enters it, a "man" occupies it. Daniel 8:13-14 described the situation as follows: "Then I heard a holy one speaking, and another holy one said to that particular one who was speaking, 'How long will the vision about the regular sacrifice apply, while the transgression causes horror, so as to allow both the holy place and the host to be trampled?' And he said to me, 'For 2300 evenings and mornings; then the holy place will be properly restored." It is properly restored when Jesus Christ enters the Holy of Holies and sits on the throne of David forever. These last two items of the job description God has given to the Jews can only be fulfilled at Jesus' second coming. This means the Jews as a nation have not been exterminated when Jesus returns. In fact, it is the Jewish people who call him back to be their Messiah. (Psalm 80, Hosea 6:1-3) In the middle of the persecution, after they flee Israel, they will repent of their sin and call on their Messiah, Jesus Christ, the son of David, to return. He will return in power as described in Revelation 19.

Therefore it follows logically that Satan would attempt to destroy the Jewish race again as he attempted to do at various times during history. Haman is recorded in the Book of Esther as having plotted to kill the Jews. If it hadn't been for the work of Mordecai, Haman would have been successful in persuading the king to kill the Jews. However, the king's wife, Esther, was also a Jew and Haman's plan would have included her death sentence as well. Queen Esther put her own life in danger by asking the king to dinner and the telling him of Haman's plot. The story ends with Haman being killed on the same gallows he had built for Mordecai. Again, Satan's plot to kill the Jews was foiled by God. Last Century, Hitler and the Nazi regime plotted to kill all the Jews as well. If the United States had not entered the war against them, the Nazis and Hitler might have won the war guaranteeing the extinction of the Jewish race. A little later in history, Stalin in Russia killed almost 50 million people, numbered among them were many Jews and Christians. This history is but a foretaste of persecutions yet to come. Those future persecutions are catalogued for us in Revelation 13. Revelation 13 is giving more specific information to explain Revelation 12:17, "Then the dragon was enraged at the woman and went off to make war against the rest of her offspring--- those who obey God's commandments and hold to the testimony of Jesus." According to Revelation 12:7, "There was war in heaven. Michael and his angels fought against the dragon, and the dragon and his angels fought back. But he was not strong enough, and they lost their place in heaven. The great dragon was hurled down---that ancient serpent called the devil, or Satan, who leads the whole world astray. He was hurled to the earth and his angels with him." The woman of Revelation 12 is the Jewish nation, Israel, which gave birth to the Messiah. Currently, in Europe and other places worldwide, anti-semitic sentiment is growing in intensity. This is Satan's Ace up his sleeve. If he can annihilate all the Jews, then there will be no Jews to call Jesus back to be their Messiah. If Jesus does not return, then Satan will remain god of this world. Jesus said that if he does not return sometime in the future, there would be no life left on the earth. (Matthew 24:22) However, Jesus promised that "this generation will certainly not pass away until all these things have happened." (Matthew 24:34) The word "generation" is a term used to describe the Jewish nation as a people group. Jesus therefore is saying Satan will be unsuccessful in annihilating the Jewish people. There will be, therefore, Jewish people alive at the end of the age to call Jesus back to be their Messiah.

There is recorded in the Old Testament the exact words the Jewish leadership will use to call their Messiah back to earth. Remember, these words are used in history when there is great animosity directed at the Jewish people. Satan has been somewhat successful in deceiving the people to hate the Jews. The context of that hatred will be Issrael's refusal to accept a world religious system that incorporates all religions into one. The False prophet of Revelation, who authors this one world religion, is the one who had the image of the Beast built and put into the Holy of Holies for the world to worship. "Then I saw another beast coming out of the earth. He had two horns like a lamb, but he spoke like a dragon. He exercised all the authority of the first beast on his behalf, and made the earth and its inhabitants worship the first beast, whose fatal wound had been healed. And he performed great and miraculous signs, even causing fire to come down from heaven in full view of men. Because of the signs he was given power to do on behalf of the first beast, he deceived the inhabitants of the earth. He ordered them to set up an image in honor of the beast who was wounded by the sword and yet lived. He was given power to give breath to the image of the first beast, so that it could speak and cause all who refused to worship the image to be killed." (Revelation 13:11-15) As an aside, it could be with all the work being done with artificial intelligence (AI), that this "image" could be a robot.

There was a conference in 1993 called the World Parliament of Religions which was attended by 6500 delegates. These world religious leaders came from all over the world to New York City. The only religious groups not invited were evangelical Denominations. This conference decided to write a new bible which would embrace all the teachings of the world religions. This conference decided that the different religions of the world were responsible for the discord and conflicts in the world. To eliminate that discord and fighting and killing among religious factions, the delegates to this conference decided it would be necessary to make all the religions into one religious system. Their rationale was that this accomplishment would usher in the peace the United Nations had been seeking for the world. One can readily see how this all fits together with Revelation 13. Satan planted the seed for a one world religion at the World Parliament of Religions. He will and is now working to bring about a one world religion. This project has one major obstacle, that being the two religions that claim to be revealed by their God.

There are two world religions that claim to be revealed; the first is Judaism coupled with Christianity. Their God is Elohim, the creator made known through Jesus Christ. (Genesis 1:1; Colossians 1:16) Islam is the second religion claiming to be revealed by its god, Allah. These two religions will reject this one world system based on the fact their religious system is based on the revelation of God. Promises to Islam that Allah will be the god of the one world religion will lure them to embrace the one world religion. Once the False Prophet begins performing signs and miracles, Islam will be melted into the mix. The Jews and Christians will not accept the one world religion. The truth of the Bible will be the authority behind their belief system. Therefore they will not accept this proposed one world religion. Jesus said there was but one road leading to eternal life and that was by faith in him and his work on the cross. Faith in what Jesus did on the cross alone is the only way to be saved from sin. Islam, though it professes to be a revealed religion, could easily be folded into a one world religion that kills those who resist it. For in their teaching the killing of the "infidel" is rewarded with special privileges in the hereafter. The reason this killing of Christians is predicted in Revelation 13 is because they will not worship the image of the Beast. Satanic deception is now leading the world towards this one world religion. Here in America, we even have individuals in our congress promoting Islam.

The Pantheistic based religions believe the world exists in a closed system. They believe, by that statement, that everything that exists is connected into one essence. Therefore they believe the tree, the animals and man are one. This truth, adherents teach, is experienced through Yoga and meditation. Yoga is practiced to neutralize the body and meditation is taught to neutralize the mind. The goal is to eliminate the body and mind from interfering with the realization of the oneness every person has with the universe. These two disciplines are therefore necessary for the body and the mind to experience Nirvana, ie. their oneness with nature and all that exists. An example of this belief system is found in the early history of the Bible where mention is made of the worship of the god Molech. This religious practice endorsed the sacrifice of children to Molech because they believed that energy was released back into this closed system through the death of a child. That additional energy was used to bring spring out of winter. This thinking abounded in agriculturally based nations. Also worshipped among agriculturally based nations was the worship of Baal. Worship of this god was the belief that sexual intercourse also released energy into this closed system enabling spring to emerge out of winter. Buds would appear on trees and plants would grow out of the soil of the earth based on how much energy could be released into this closed Pantheistic system. Therefore in the temples of these religions there would be male and female prostitutes with whom worshippers could engage in sexual activities. This is why so much sexual immorality is mentioned to exist among the seven churches listed in Revelation 2-3. These religious practices were encountered when the Israelites lived in Egypt, then later as they traveled towards the land God had promised Israel. God warned the Israelites through Moses not to engage in any of the religious practices of those nations. In fact, the Ten Commandments given by God for his people to observe were directed towards not having any other Gods other than Jahweh, the God who miraculously brought them out of Egypt. Even so the men of Israel were seduced by the prostitutes of Baal when passing near Moab. Balaam told the king of Moab, Balak, that God would punish the Israelites if he was successful in tempting the men of Israel to worship Baal by having intercourse with their prostitutes. And that is exactly what happened.

Satan has sown much deception through the idea of Pantheism. The Apostle Paul had to address the deception in the church at Corinth over the idea that meat offered to idols in the temple worship somehow contaminated the meat. Because of Pantheistic teaching, the thought was that the meat offered to gods in the form of animal sacrifices were one with that god and thus to eat it was to fellowship with that god and worship it. What was true of most idolatrous temples was that there was a meat market attached to the temple. Meat from the animal sacrifices were either consumed there in the temple or sold at the attached meat market to the public. That is where this meat became available for sale. This is the meat being questioned by the Christians in Corinth. The Apostle Paul wrote to them that Zeus was not a real god and therefore sacrifices offered to him in the temple were offered to nothing. Therefore they were not to believe that they were worshipping a god by eating the meat offered at the temple. (1 Corinthian 8)

The ordinances of Baptism and the Lord's Supper (Communion) were given to the church to be observed "in remembrance of me", Jesus said in Luke 22:19-20. These ordinances represent what Jesus said in John 14:20, "On that day you will realize that I am in my Father, and I in you and you in me." The phrase "you in me" is represented by baptism when symbolically we are place in Christ by being dipped into the water. The phrase "I in you" symbolically occurs when we take the bread and cup and eat and drink them. The symbols at communion represent the body and blood of our Lord Jesus Christ. They are not literally the body and blood of Jesus Christ. They do not become the body or blood of Christ when a Catholic Priest holds up the elements during Communion. Transubstantiation is taught by the Catholic Church whereby they believe the elements become the real body and blood of Christ. This is where Pantheistic teaching has crept into the Catholic Church in their doctrine of transubstantiation. The Apostle Paul answered the question about Pantheistic thinking in 1 Corinthians 11:12, "For as the woman came from man, so also man is born of a woman. But everything comes from God." God is not part or "one" with his creation, but distinct from it. The Hebrew word for create in Genesis One is <u>Barah,</u> which means to bring something into existence that which did not before exist. He created by uttering the words and brought into existence things that did not exist before he created them. They exist because it was his will to create them, but he is not "one" in essence with them. Colossians and Romans both speak of God holding all of his creation together. Every atom, every molecule in the entire universe is held together according to his will. However, he exists separately from it. God is transcendent as opposed to imminent relative to all that he brought into existence. God said of himself, "I am God and not a man." (Hosea 11:9) That statement said it all. God is not "one" with his creation. He is separate from it.

Satan has tried to deceive and confuse the church about his role in history. Like God said to the church at Sardis, "Wake up." (Revelation 3:2) To the church at Ephesus God said we wage war with Satan and his fallen host. Therefore, "Pray." (Ephesians 6:18) This Chapter provides a number of prayer requests you can make knowing Satan's strategy and the work he is attempting to accomplish.

Questions:

1. What hope does the Book of Esther provide for your life as a Christian?

_____

_____

_____

2. Describe the failures of Satan to eliminate the "he" of Genesis 3:15.

_____

_____

_____

3. How has this Chapter made you more aware of the need to follow world events?

_____

_____

_____

4. Why does Revelations 12 now make sense in light of Satan's plan to destroy the Jews?

_____

_____

_____

5. Review Daniel 9:24 and explain what God wants the Jewish people to accomplish before he returns.

_____

_____

_____

6. What new insights have you gained from Daniel 9:24?

_____

_____

_____

7. What information in this Chapter seems to stand out as very important to know?

_____

_____

_____

8. Read again Leviticus 16. What is so special about the Day of Atonement (Yom Kippur)?

_____

_____

_____

9. Describe the meaning of the ordinances of Baptism and Communion.

_____

_____

_____

Chapter Nine

It is during the Seventieth week of Daniel or last seven years of that prophecy, that the Jewish people accomplish the task God gave them in Daniel 9:24. Remember, the prophecy to Daniel was for 70 sevens weeks of years. (Daniel 9:24-27) Seven and sixty-two of those weeks of years were fulfilled when the Messiah rode on a donkey into Jerusalem and then later was killed. God's time clock finished ticking on that first Palm Sunday. It began with the return of Nehemiah to Jerusalem in 445 B.C. when the Persian king, Artaxerxes, gave Nehemiah permission to return to Jerusalem and rebuild the walls. (Nehemiah 2:1-10) It stopped ticking after sixty-nine of the weeks expired when Jesus rode into Jerusalem and offered the kingdom to God's people assembled there. A kingdom has three parts to it. It has a king, a right to rule and the people who are ruled. Jesus was the king of the kingdom while the people of the kingdom were the Jewish people in Jerusalem at the time of his entry to the city on Palm Sunday. The only thing missing was his right to rule, which he would later establish on the cross. That right to rule is found in John 3:16, "For God so loved the world that he gave his only begotten son, that whosoever believes in him, should not perish, but have everlasting life."

The final seven years of the seventieth week of Daniel start God's time clock to begin ticking again when a "peace treaty" is signed between Israel and the "he" of Daniel 9:27. This pronoun grammatically refers back to "the people of the ruler who will come and destroy the city and the temple." (Daniel 9:26) The nation to which this refers is the Roman nation and its army which captured the city of Jerusalem and destroyed the temple in 70 A.D. (Daniel 9:26) The angel Gabriel, who gave God's revelation to Daniel, informed Daniel that a "he" would come from that nation and "confirm a covenant with many for the last seven years period of time. In the middle of the seventieth week he will put an end to sacrifice and offering. And on a wing of the temple, he will set up an abomination that causes desolation, until the end that is decreed is poured out on him." (Daniel 9:27)

The Bible predicts this "he" will come from out of the Beast, which is a revival of the old Roman government. In fact, Revelation 17:9-12, teaches this "he" is said to be an eighth king: "This calls for a mind with wisdom. The seven heads are seven hills on which the woman sits. They are also seven kings. Five have fallen, one is, the other is yet to come; but when he does come, he must remain for a little while. The beast who once was, and now is not, is an eighth king. He belongs to the seven and is going to his destruction. The ten horns you saw are ten kings who have not yet received a kingdom, but who for one hour will receive authority as kings alongside the beast. They have one purpose and will give their power and authority to the beast. They will make war against the Lamb, but the Lamb will overcome them because he is Lord of Lords and King of Kings---and with him will be his chosen and faithful followers."

This "he" is the anti-Christ who comes out of the beast. The beast has seven heads and ten horns. The seven heads are kings with kingdoms. Five of those kingdoms have existed in history but are no longer existing kingdoms or nations that ruled the world. They have ceased to exist. The sixth kingdom exists at the time the Apostle John is writing the book called Revelation. The five kingdoms that once existed are nations that once conquered vast areas of world. The first nation being referred to is Assyria. (2 Kings) They were followed by Egypt, the second head. (Exodus) The third head was the Babylonian empire led by Nebachadnezzer. (Damiel 1-6) The fourth was the Medo-Persian empire led by Artexerxes. (Esther) The fifth kingdom was the Greek empire under Alexander the Great. "Then a mighty king will appear, who will rule with great power and do as he pleases. After he has appeared, his kingdom will be broken up and parceled out toward the four winds of heaven. It will not go to his descendents, nor will it have the power he exercised, because his empire will be uprooted and given to others." (Daniel 11:3-4) History records that after Alexander the Great died, his four generals each took a portion of the empire he had created through his conquests.

The Greek empire was followed by the Roman Empire, the sixth head. The Apostle John, when writing about this sixth head wrote "One of the heads of the beast seemed to have had a fatal wound, but the fatal wound had been healed." The Roman Empire ceased to exist in history in 454 A.D. when the Visigoths attacked Rome and destroyed it. When the Apostle John is looking ahead at history yet to come, he looks from that vantage point (about 90 A.D.) and writes about the sixth head writing that "it is", meaning that it existed at the time of his writing. However, The Apostle John also used the phrase "it was" which indicated that it no longer existed at some future point in history. The Apostle John is writing around 90 A.D. when he wrote Revelation. Therefore he is predicting the future about Rome, the empire that was a world-wide power that then ruled over Judea. The phrase, "it was," means that as the Apostle John looked ahead in history, he was predicting the future demise of the Roman Empire. When the Apostle John skips ahead in history towards its conclusion, he used the term "will come" referring to the beast as consisting of a Roman type government. In the Roman government at the time of John's writing there existed an emperor and a Senate. The beast that will come will have a similar type of government consisting of the anti-Christ filling the role of the emperor and the ten kings filling the role the Senate played in the then Roman Empire. Therefore he describes the beast as "now is". The Apostle John is therefore predicting that another world government will come into power. This is what Adolf Hitler wanted to achieve and this was why the United Nations was formed after World War Two. It was formed to keep a world government like what Adolf Hitler was trying to build from ever being formed.

The "beast" then is a world government that will be formed sometime in the future. The phrase "will come" is the Apostle John's prediction of the beast. Revelation 13:1-10 gives the following description of the beast, "And I saw. . ." Revelation 13 does not begin with "And the dragon stood on the shore of the sea." Early manuscript evidence places this statement at the end of Revelation 12. Therefore, the description of the beast begins in Revelation 13:1-10, "And I saw a beast coming out of the sea. He had ten horns and seven heads, with ten crowns on his horns, and on each head a blasphemous name. The beast I saw resembled a leopard, but had feet like those of a bear and a mouth like that of a lion. The dragon (Revelation 12:2, 9, 13) gave the beast his power and his throne and great authority. One of the heads of the beast seemed to have had a fatal wound, but the wound had been healed. This was discussed earlier in this book. The whole world was astonished and followed the beast." One reason for the world's allegiance was that the beast had been able to kill the two witnesses that previously were ministering for God in Jerusalem. These two men, probably Elijah and Moses, indicated by the things they were able to do, could not be harmed or killed after attempts were made to do so. Those events transpired during the first half of the Seventieth Week of Daniel, or 3 ½ years. Revelation 11:2-13 gives clarity to these events, "But exclude the outer court; do not measure it, because it has been given to the Gentiles. They will trample on the holy city for 42 months. And I will give power to my two witnesses, and they will prophecy for 1200 days clothed in sackcloth. These are the two olive trees and the two lampstands that stand before the Lord of the earth. If anyone tries to harm them, fire comes from their mouths and devours their enemies. This is how anyone who wants to harm them must die. These men have the power to turn the water into blood and to strike the earth with every kind of plague as often as they want. Now when they have finished their testimony, the beast that comes from the Abyss will attack them, and overpower and kill them. Their bodies will lie in the street of the great city, which is figuratively called Sodom and Egypt, where their Lord was crucified. For three and a half days men from every people, tribe, language, and nation will gaze on their bodies and refuse them burial. The inhabitants of the earth will gloat over them and celebrate by sending each other gifts, because these two prophets had tormented those who live on the earth. But after the three and a half days a breath of life from God entered them, and they stood on their feet, and terror struck those who saw them. Then they heard a loud voice from heaven saying to them, 'Come up here'. And they went up to heaven in a cloud while their enemies looked on. At that very hour there was a severe earthquake and a tenth of the city collapsed. Seven thousand people were killed in the earthquake, and the survivors were terrified and gave glory to the God of heaven."

That phrase "gave glory to God" was an Old Testament expression meaning they became believers. They became believers in the God of heaven being proclaimed by the two witnesses. Who were these inhabitants of Jerusalem who became Christians when the two witnesses were taken to heaven? I believe they are the 144,000 Jewish young men, 12,000 from each of the twelve tribes of Israel. Revelation 7:2-17 describes these men and the protection God gave them. This protection was needed since immediately after the anti-Christ killed the two witnesses, the great persecution predicted by

Jesus in Matthew 24:15-22 began. Immediately after killing the two witnesses, the anti-Christ stopped the sacrifices from being offered in the temple. Instead, the world was to worship his image in the temple, and anyone who refused was to be killed. Therefore the 144.000 needed God's protection as they went out and evangelized the world for the last time before Christ's kingdom would be established here on earth. "Then I saw another angel coming up from the east, having the seal of the living God. He called out in a loud voice to the four angels who had been given power to harm the land and the sea. 'Do not harm the land or the sea or the trees until we put a seal on the foreheads of the servants of our God. Then I heard the number of those who were sealed: 144,000 from all the tribes of Israel...After this I looked and there before me was a great multitude that no one could count, from every nation, tribe, people and language, standing before the throne and in front of the Lamb. They were wearing white robes and were holding palm branches in their hands. And they cried out in a loud voice: 'Salvation belongs to our God, who sits on the throne and to the Lamb.'...Then one of the elders asked me, 'These in white robes---who are they and where did they come from?' I answered, 'Sir, you know.' And he said, 'These are they who have come out of the great tribulation; they have washed their robes and made them white in the blood of the Lamb. Therefore, they are before the throne of God and serve him day and night in his temple; and he who sits on the throne will spread his tent over them. Never again will they hunger; never again will they thirst. He sun will not beat on them nor any scorching heat. For the Lamb at the center of the throne will be their shepherd; he will lead them to springs of living water. And God will wipe away every tear from their eyes.'"

The text continued with these words, "Men worshipped the dragon because he had given authority to the beast, and they also worshipped the beast and asked, 'Who can wage war against him?' The beast was given a mouth to utter proud words and blasphemies and to exercise his authority for forty-two months. He opened his mouth to blaspheme God, and to slander his name and his dwelling place and those who live in heaven. He was given power to make war against the saints and to conquer them. And he was given authority over every tribe, people, language and nation. All inhabitants of the earth will worship the beast---all whose names have not been written in the book of life belonging to the Lamb that was slain from the creation of the world."

It is written of the beast that it had ten horns. The horns had crowns which had not been given to them when Revelation was written. The "crowns" represent rulers or kings, leaders of those ten nations. The symbolism is clear. The beast, a revival of the old Roman Empire, has ten kings that corporately rule the world alongside the anti-Christ and have given their authority to the beast. When the Apostle John looked ahead at this new world government, he noticed that it had been divided into ten areas all ruled by their respective leaders called "kings". The crowns symbolize that those kings have the authority over the people they represent. The Bible says that these so called kings have given their authority to the beast. There is a commission in Washington D.C. that has the plans for dividing the world into ten sections or territories. Canada, Mexico and the United States constitute one of those ten divisions. China will be the glue that holds this future conglomeration together. They are already a threat to the value of the Dollar. The references in the news and from elsewhere speak of plans for a global economy and a one world government. There is already a one world court. The American Patriot Forum on January 17, 2021, featured an article entitled "Facebook Censors Mexican Cardinal." In the article, Cardinal Juan Sandoval Igniquez was identified as the Cardinal censored for denouncing the New World Order. This was done even though Pope Francis, on March 17, 2021, said much the same thing as Facebook. Pope Francis was quoted as saying, "The world will never be the same again. But it is precisely within this calamity (referring to Covd 19) that we must grasp those signs which may prove to be the cornerstone of reconstruction...by building a new world order on solidarity." This new reality, welcomed by the Pope, will advance the left's agenda to impose socialism on the world. The idea of globalization has been at the center of world thinking for some time. It is the hope of the "left" in our political structure to achieve goals that eventuate in the U.S.A. joining such an organization.

The fact that the world leaders want this kind of world and are working towards its establishment is discovered from the words written in Revelation 13. In this Scripture, God is describing how the economy in the future will work. "He also forced everyone, small and great, rich and poor, free and slave, to receive a mark on their forehead or right hand, so that no one could buy or sell unless he had the mark, which is the name of the beast or the number of his name. This calls for wisdom. If anyone has insight, let him calculate the number of the beast, for it is man's number. His number is 666." Today, our credit cards have three sets of four numbers each. I imagine a credit card with three sets of six numbers would cover the number of people on the earth. Not only is this number necessary to conduct any kind of business or grocery shopping, it serves many other purposes as well. For example, it identifies the whereabouts of the person submitting the number to make a transaction. No person will be able to hide from this world government. No one will be able to exceed the amount of money they have in the world bank for any transaction, because the computer governing these transactions will have a detailed account of their financial condition. That will not only eliminate the possibility of going into debt since the computer governing all transactions will decline the person's purchase if they have no money to cover it. Under this system, workers would have their paychecks automatically deposited and taxes would be taken out at the discretion of the government.

Talk about Big Government and control. This is where our world leaders want to take us. They want us to be completely dependent on them and in the process, remove our liberty. Under the administrations of President Clinton and President Obama, The United States was being carefully maneuvered towards this end. The NAFTA treaty weakened America financially. Those presidents as well as President Bush weakened America giving Europe and China our manufacturing jobs. They signed treaties with China guaranteeing its wealth at the expense of America and deceitfully tried to hide the motive of their actions. The reason President Trump was so hated was that he was not in the brotherhood of these politicians. His motto of "Make America Great Again" was totally against what these other politicians were trying to do to America. President Obama deliberately made us weak militarily so we would not be able to compete on the international stage. Donald Trump began changing all of that. He made us energy independent. He began to change our economy so unemployment began to fall. He gave hope to the Black community with "opportunity zones", prison reforms, school choice and much more. He stood up to China, the European Community and NATO. He increased our military might. America resumed its place as a leader among the nations. That is why the "left" in this country hated President Trump so much. He threw a "wrench" into the work of the "Progressives." The more he loved this country and tried to work for it, the more they hated him. To them, he was keeping us from our appointment with destiny. That destiny is described by Mark Levin in his latest book, "American Marxism."

Who is behind all this? This book has been explaining the answer to this question. Now we have as a President, one who wants to reinitiate the goals of the "left" and change the direction our country was moving towards under President Trump. President Biden, by his attitude towards immigrants, our economy, our energy, our military, China etc., wants us weak and dependent on the nations of the world. He wants us to embrace the socialistic system of the world. He wants to take away our guns so there is no way we can revolt against the governmental system he and the Democrats are trying to create. What can be done? Remember, behind all this is Satan, trying to maintain his position as god. Therefore, we can pray, is the answer to the afore-mentioned question. Remember the disciples when Jesus sent them out recorded in Luke 10. They came back astonished that "even the demons are subject to us in your name." Christians have lost sight of the power and authority they have as children of the King of Kings and Lord of Lords. In the Upper Room before Jesus died and rose again, he told his disciples to receive the Holy Spirit he was going to give them to continue his work here until he returned. Therefore be filled with the Spirit of God and pray for our country to turn back from its trust in everything but God. To the church at Corinth, God said through the Apostle Paul not to trust "in the wisdom of this age or the rulers of this age." (1Corinthians 2:6) Our world is crying out for Barabbas instead of the loving and holy God revealed in Christ Jesus our Lord. Therefore pray that the demons responsible for the deception gripping our nation and the world be silenced. You occupy a position whereby you can ask the Lord anything according to his will and he will do it. (John 14:13-14) Pray therefore that he send these demons to Hell!

Humanism reaches its zenith when an image of a man is put into the Holy of Holies at the temple in Jerusalem and the world worships it. That is what the Apostle John predicted when he wrote these words, "And he performed great and miraculous signs, even causing fire to come down from heaven to earth in full view of men. Because of the signs he was given power to do on behalf of the first beast, he deceived the inhabitants of the earth. He ordered them to set up an image in honor of the beast who was wounded by the sword and yet lived. He was given power to give breath to the image of the first beast so that it could speak and cause all who refused to worship the beast to be killed." (Revelation 13:13-15) This statement is no longer far-fetched. Just look at the technology they have incorporated into the automobile. They now have sensors to detect an animal or person in front of the car and can bring it to a stop. They now have sensors to detect a lane change. They have cars to deliver your groceries. Soon, the predictions are, there will no longer be privately owned vehicles. Instead, one simply calls for a car with the destination determined, and it will arrive in your driveway. There will no longer be a need for gas. With the new technology for electrical power in the new batteries being developed, there will not be the need for gas stations. Technology is changing our society daily. The new computer chips are extremely fast and are eliminating many jobs. Many stores cannot survive and are going out of business. They even today have computer chips that can read contracts and explain them to a person in need of a lawyer. That occupation will soon be eliminated with the growth of our progress. Therefore, when the Bible speaks of some kind of computerized droid that can speak, it is possible since that kind of instrument exists today.

Questions:

1. Do you think when God calls to his two witnesses with the words "Come up here," that that summons could coincide with the Rapture of the Church? (1 Thessalonians 4:13-18) Why or why not?

    _____

    _____

    _____

2. Read Luke 10:1ff. Do you think Christians have that same kind of authority today?

    _____

    _____

    _____

3. What does Jesus mean by "all authority" in Matthew 28:18? Do you have it?

    _____

    _____

    _____

4. Read Matthew 21:23-25 Why is authority the key thought here?

    _____

    _____

    _____

5. What are the pros and cons of socialism vs. capitalism? What does the Bible teach?

    _____

    _____

    _____

6   Why is socialism so important for a "new world order" to exist?

_____

_____

_____

7. What is the definition of "humanism" and how do the 10 Commandments address it?

_____

_____

_____

8. How has your understanding of the "beast" of Revelation changed, if at all?

_____

_____

_____

9. What do you see occurring in the world that would lead to a one world religion?

_____

_____

_____

Chapter Ten

"What in the world is happening" is the title of this book. Are you aware that The Hamas has been bombarding Israel with rockets and mortars at the time of this writing? Lebanon has also joined the attack. Do you recall that under President Richard Nixon a similar conflict caused Russia to prepare to invade this area of the world under the guise of stopping the conflict? It was only President Nixon taking our country's military readiness to a certain Depth Com that Russia backed down. Imagine with me that Russia did today what it proposed to do some 50 years ago. Many Bible teachers belief the invasion of Russia precludes the beginning of the Seventieth Week Prophecy recorded in Daniel 9:24-27. I share this to reveal how current events could easily catapult us into end time prophecies being fulfilled.

The Scriptures being fulfilled if that happened are to be found in Ezekiel 36-39. Specifically, in Ezekiel 38:14-23, "Therefore son of man, prophecy and say to Gog: This is what the Sovereign Lord says: In that day, when my people Israel are living in safety, will you not take notice of it? You will come from your place in the far north, you and many nations with you, all of them riding on horses, a great horde, a mighty army. You will advance against my people Israel like a cloud that covers the land. (Clearly a reference to paratroopers) In days to come, O Gog, I will bring you against my land, so that the nations may know me when I show myself holy through you before their eyes...This is what will happen in that day: When Gog attacks the land of Israel, my hot anger will be aroused, declares the Sovereign Lord. In my zeal and fiery wrath, I declare at that time there shall be a great earthquake in the land of Israel. The fish of the sea, the birds of the air, the beasts of the field, every creature that moves along the ground, and all the people on the face of the earth will tremble at my presence. The mountains will be overturned, the cliffs will crumble and every wall will fall to the ground. I will summon a sword against Gog on all my mountains, declares the Sovereign Lord. Every man's sword will be against his brother. I will execute judgment upon him with plague and bloodshed. I will pour down torrents of rain, hailstones and burning sulfur on him and on his troops and on the many nations with him. (Is this a reference to Atomic warfare? There sure is one in Zechariah 14:12, "This is the plague with which the Lord will strike all nations that fought against Jerusalem. Their flesh will rot while they are standing on their feet, their eyes will rot in their sockets and their tongues will rot in their mouths. And I will show my greatness and holiness, and I will make myself known in the sight of many nations. Then they will know I am the Lord." I am writing these things to open our eyes to how quickly these scriptures could be fulfilled in our own day, even tomorrow.

Before this prophecy in Ezekiel could be fulfilled, it was necessary for Israel to have become a nation. Isaiah the prophet foretold how this future event would occur in Isaiah 66:6 when the following question was posed, "Can a country be born in a day or a nation be brought forth in a moment?" The answer to that question is a resounding "yes"! On May 15th, 1948, the United Nations voted to create a land for the nation of Israel to occupy. The "dry bones" prophecy recorded in Ezekiel 37:1ff began to be fulfilled. Notice what the text communicates, explaining how this happened. "The hand of the Lord was upon me and he brought me out by the

Spirit of the Lord and set me in the middle of the valley; it was full of bones. He led me back and forth among them, and I saw a great many bones on the floor of the valley, bones that were very dry. He asked me, 'Son of man, can these bones live?' I said, 'O Sovereign Lord, you alone know.' Then he said to me, 'Prophecy to these bones and say to them, 'Dry bones, hear the word of the Lord! This is what the Sovereign Lord says to these bones. I will make breath enter you and you will come to life. I will attach tendons to you and make flesh come upon you and cover you with skin: I will put breath in you and you will come to life. Then you will know that I am the Lord.'"

That skeleton is the nation of Israel. "Then he said to me, 'Son of man, these bones are the whole house of Israel." (Ezekiel 37:11) Israel lives in the land called Israel today by the will of God. God has restored Israel to the land given to its patriarch, Abraham. (Genesis 12:1-3) They will remain in the land now and until the Abomination of Desolation occurs, a prophecy made by Jesus in Matthew 24:15-22. At the time of the Abomination of Desolation, Jesus instructed the inhabitants of Jerusalem and Israel to flee their country. Jesus explained the reason for the exodus with these words, "So when you see standing in the holy place the abomination that causes desolation, spoken of through the prophet Daniel--let the reader understand---then let those who are in Judea flee to the mountains. Let no one on the roof of his house go down to take anything out of his house. Let no one in the field go back to get his cloak. How dreadful it will be in those days for a pregnant woman and nursing mothers! Pray that your flight will not take place in winter or on the Sabbath. For then there will be a great distress, unequalled from the beginning of the world until now---and never to be equaled again. If those days had not been cut short, no one would survive, but for the sake of the elect those days will be shortened." If one thought that the Holocaust, the attempted systematic annihilation of the Jewish race by Adolph Hitler, was horrific, then take notice about what Jesus predicted will happen in Israel to the Jewish people at a certain point in time in the future. Jesus said the anti-Christ would stop the daily sacrifices in the temple and replace the reverence once held for the Holy of Holies in the temple. Instead of worshipping the God of Israel who promised to dwell among his people there, the people will be instructed to worship an image of the anti-Christ there in the Holy of Holies. He will not only disallow any future worship of the God of Israel, but will kill anyone who attempts to do so.

The reason for this assault on Jerusalem and the Jews is the same as indicated earlier in this book. Satan wants to remain god of this earth and will do anything to retain that position. Therefore, he has to destroy every Jew on the face of the earth. If there are no Jews, then they cannot call Jesus back to be their Messiah. Jesus said he would not return until the Jews did so. (Matthew 23:37-39) When the Jews flee Judea and Jerusalem, Jesus told them to flee to the mountains. East of Judea is Syria and Jordan. The Bible teaches that the anti-Christ will chase the Jews out of Israel into those mountains east of Israel. Revelation 12:7-9, 13-17 teach this from the writings of the Apostle John, "And there was war in heaven. Michael and his angels fought against the Dragon, and the Dragon and his angels fought back. But he was not strong enough, and they lost their place in heaven. The great dragon was hurled down---that ancient serpent called the devil or Satan, who leads the whole world astray. He was hurled to the earth, and his angels with him. Satan is manipulating current events and establishing a mindset among the nations that will lead history to a point when the anti-Christ will rule in Jerusalem as an extension of the "beast". This position of authority will enable him to launch an attack on the Jews with an intensity not experienced in past history. (Matthew 24:21)

One of the events leading up to the Abomination that make Desolate (Matthew 24:15) is described in Revelation 12 when Satan is thrown out of heaven. "When the dragon saw that he had been hurled to the earth, he pursued the woman who had given birth to the male child. The woman was given the two wings of a great eagle, so that she might fly to the place prepared for her in the desert, where she would be taken care of for a time, times and half a time, out of the reach of the serpent. Then from his mouth the serpent spewed water like a river, to overtake the woman and sweep her away with the torrent. But the earth opened its mouth and helped the woman by swallowing the river that the dragon had spewed out of his mouth. Then the dragon was enraged at the woman and went off to wage war with the rest of her offspring--- those who obey God's commandments and hold to the testimony of Jesus." (Revelation 12:13-17)

The place in the desert to which they flee is a place called Bozrah, located in Eden, now present day Jordan. A Christian businessman sprinkled this area with Bibles some years ago in anticipation of this event. This area may seem familiar to you because there are many pictures taken of this walled city. One of the films Harrison Ford starred in as Indiana Jones was filmed in this city of Bozrah. We know that this is where the Jewish people will flee to after leaving Israel because this is the place Jesus returns to when the Jews call him back to be their Messiah. (Isaiah 63:1ff) When he returns, remember that the world has gathered to destroy the Jews at the direction of the anti-Christ. The battle that ensues is very bloody as the Lord Jesus Christ defends his people. Revelation 14:20 describes the battle as follows: "And threw them into the winepress of God's wrath. They were trampled in the winepress outside the city and blood flowed out of the press, rising as high as the horses' bridle for a distance of 1600 Stadia." (About 180 miles) The prophet Isaiah comments further on this future event. Isaiah 63:1 begins with this question, "Who is this coming from Eden, from Bozrah, with his garments stained crimson? Who is this, robed in splendor, striding forward in the greatness of his strength? 'It is I, speaking in righteousness, mighty to save.' Why are your garments red, like those of one treading the winepress? 'I have trodden the winepress alone; from the nations no one was with me. I trampled them in my anger and trod them down in my wrath; their blood spattered on my garments, and I stained all my clothing. For the day of vengeance was in my heart, and the year of my redemption has come...I trampled the nations in my anger; in my wrath I made them drunk and poured their blood on the ground.'" A parallel passage to this one is found in Isaiah 34:7-8 which reads as follows: "For the Lord has a sacrifice in Bozrah and a great slaughter in Edom...Their land will be drenched with blood and the dust will be soaked with fat. The Lord has a day of vengeance, a year of retribution, to uphold Zion's cause."

A New Testament passage also describing this event is found in Revelation 19:11-16. There we read, "I saw heaven standing open and there before me was a white horse, whose rider is called Faithful and True. With justice he judges and makes war. His eyes are like blazing fire, and on his head are many crowns. He has a name written on him that no one knows but he himself. He is dressed in a robe dipped in blood, and his name is the Word of God. The armies of heaven were following him, riding on white horses and dressed in fine linen, white and clean. Out of his mouth comes a sharp sword with which to strike down the nations. He will rule them with an iron scepter. He treads the winepress of the fury of the wrath of God Almighty. On his robe and on his thigh he has this name written: KING OF KINGS AND LORD OF LORDS." The backdrop for this action taken by our Lord and Savior Jesus Christ is found in Revelation 16:12-16. "The sixth angel poured out his bowl on the great river Euphrates, and its water was dried up to prepare the way for the kings from the East. Then I saw three evil spirits that looked like frogs; they came out of the mouth of the dragon, out of the mouth of the beast and out of the mouth of the false prophet. They are spirits of demons performing miraculous signs, and they go out to the kings of the whole world, to gather them for the battle of the great day of God Almighty...Then they gathered the kings together to the place that in Hebrew is called Armageddon." The nations are coming because they have been deceived to believe that the Jews are causing the New World Order from being completely conceived. They have been told that all the wealth of Israel will be theirs as a part of this New World Order. Speculation about the wealth of Israel is said to be found in the Dead Sea, composed of chemicals estimated to be of more value than all the wealth harvested on earth to that point. The top soil in the Jordan Valley is six feet deep. This allows Israel to feed much of Europe its vegetables and fruits. What these nations are not told is that Satan is behind this invitation to come to Israel and destroy the Jewish people. He wants them completely annihilated so he can remain god of this world. For remember Jesus words, that if the Jews do not call him back to be their Messiah, he is not returning to earth as the Jewish Messiah to sit on the throne of David. (Matthew 23:37-39) These Scriptures give us an overview of things to come and the rationale behind them.

One cannot understand fully what life will be like when the "man of lawlessness", the anti-Christ , is demanding the world worship him and his image in the Holy of Holies. 2 Thessalonians 2:4-12 describes this man of lawlessness as follows: "He will oppose and will exalt himself over everything that is called God or is worshipped, so that he sets himself up in God's temple, proclaiming himself to be God. Don't you remember that when I was with you I used to tell you these things? And now you know what is holding him back, so that he may be revealed at the proper time. For the secret power of lawlessness is already at work: but the one who now holds it back will continue to do so till he is taken out of the way. And then the lawless one will be revealed whom the Lord Jesus will overthrow with the breath of his mouth and destroy by the splendor of his coming. The coming of the lawless one will be in accordance with the work of Satan displayed in all kinds of

131

counterfeit miracles, sign and wonders, and in every sort of evil that deceives those who are perishing. They perish because they refuse to love the truth and so be saved. For this reason God sends them a powerful delusion so they will believe the lie and so that all will be condemned who have not believed the truth, but have delighted in wickedness." This wickedness is said here to express itself in every sort of evil. Imagine a world where there is no moral restraint but instead exhibits the behavior promoted by the Devil through the anti-Christ. It will be a world full of anarchy and orgies. Revelation 17 describes what the environment in the world and in Jerusalem will be like when the anti-Christ is ruling from the Holy of Holies in Jerusalem: "One of the seven angels who had the seven bowls came and said to me, 'Come, I will show you the punishment of the great prostitute, who sits on many waters. With her the kings of the earth committed adultery and the inhabitants of the earth were intoxicated with the wine of her adulteries.' Then the angel carried me away in the Spirit into the desert. There I saw a woman sitting on a scarlet beast that was covered with blasphemous names and had seven heads and ten horns. The woman was dressed in purple and scarlet, and was glittering with gold, precious stones and pearls. She held a golden cup in her hand filled with abominable things and the filth of her adulteries. This title was written on her forehead: MYSTERY BABYLON THE GREAT THE MOTHER OF PROSTITUTES AND OF THE ABOMINATIONS OF THE EARTH. I saw that the woman was drunk with the blood of the saints, the blood of those who bore testimony to Jesus. When I saw her I was greatly astonished. Then the angel said to me, 'Why are you astonished? I will explain to you the mystery of the woman and the beast she rides, which has the seven heads and the ten horns. The beast, which you saw, once was, and now is not and will come up out of the Abyss and go to his destruction. The inhabitants of the earth whose names have not been written in the book of life from the creation of the world will be astonished when they see the beast, because he once was , now is not, and yet will come.' This calls for a mind with wisdom. The seven heads are seven hills on which the woman sits. They are also seven kings. Five have fallen, one is , the other has not yet come, but when he does come, he must remain for a little while. The beast who once was, and now is not, is an eighth king. He belongs to the seven and is going to his destruction. The ten horns you saw are ten kings who have not yet received a kingdom, but who for one hour will receive authority as kings along with the beast. They have one purpose and will give their authority and power to the beast. They will make war against the Lamb, but the Lamb will overcome them because he is Lord of Lords and King of Kings---and with him will be his called chosen and faithful followers. Then the angel said to me, 'The waters you saw, where the prostitute sits, are peoples, multitudes, nations and languages. The beast and the ten horns you saw will hate the prostitute. They will bring her to ruin and leave her naked; they will eat her flesh and burn her with fire. For God has put it into their hearts to accomplish his purpose by agreeing to give the beast their power to rule, until God's words are fulfilled. The woman you saw is the great city that rules over the kings of the earth.'"

The city where the anti-Christ dwells is the city of Jerusalem, where the temple is that houses the Holy of Holies. Instead of being a city of "peace" as described in its name, it will be a city where all kinds of abominations are occurring and being promoted. Any attempt to worship anyone other than the anti-Christ will be met with the force of unparalleled rage from the Devil himself. People who worship anyone other than the Devil, reflected in the person of the anti-Christ, will be killed. The Scriptures cited earlier in this Chapter support what is being written about the environment existing in Jerusalem at the time of the beast's rule in Jerusalem. Today in America one can watch cities fall under the control of anarchists who rape, kill, plunder and fire-bomb citizens of those communities because they have little to no police presence to fight against these mobs. These cities have no authority to resist the anarchy because they have reduced the numbers of police in their city. Law and order is fast becoming a dull memory. Multiply that picture hundreds of times to get a flavor of what the "harlot" will bring to Jerusalem, Israel and the world during the last three and one-half years of history prior to the Lord's return. Jesus said, "Then you will be handed over to be persecuted and put to death, and you will be hated by all nations because of me." (Matthew 24:9)

Questions:

1. Can all of history be explained by the meaning of Genesis 3:15? Explain!

   _____

   _____

   _____

2. What are some historical evidences that Satan wants to keep his title of god?

   _____

   _____

   _____

3. What has Jesus done to take away Satan's position of god of this world?

   _____

   _____

   _____

4. What does Satan believe will secure a permanent position for him as "god of this world?" (2 Corinthians 4:4)

   _____

   _____

   _____

5. Could the fulfillment of Revelation 12:7ff coincide with the activity of the two witnesses and their death recorded in Revelation 11?

   _____

   _____

   _____

6. Is it difficult to reconcile the image of the King of Kings and Lord of Lords with a sword killing the enemies of Christianity and the image of Jesus in the Gospels compassionately feeding the 5000, healing the sick, raising the dead and saying "Come unto me you who are heavy laden and I will give you rest"?

    _____

    _____

    _____

7. How difficult is it for you to think of Jerusalem as the woman called Babylon the Great, the "mother of prostitutes and of the abominations of the earth?" (Revelation 17:5)

    _____

    _____

    _____

8. Describe a world under the authority of the Anti-Christ!

    _____

    _____

    _____

Chapter Eleven

The earth will be a gruesome place to live during the last three and one-half years prior to the Second Coming of Jesus Christ. The anarchy and injustices people will experience are hard to fathom. The only redeeming quality of this time period will be the 144,000 Jewish youths witnessing to the grace of God. (Revelation 7, 14) They will be spared death at the hands of the Beast and Anti-Christ because of the protective mark God placed upon them. (Revelation 7:3) They sang a song only they knew and preached the eternal gospel saying, "Fear God and give him glory." This is what they had expressed after the two witnesses were taken up to heaven and a great earthquake had occurred in Jerusalem. (Revelation 11:13) They were sealed and preached the Gospel to the whole earth. This is what Jesus had predicted would happen in Matthew 24:14. The result of their preaching was many came to faith in Jesus as their Lord and Savior. Even though this faith in Christ would mean death at the hands of the Beast and Anti-Christ, a large multitude believed anyway. Revelation 6:9 reveals a portion of their number, "When the Lamb opened the fifth seal, I saw under the altar the souls of those who had been slain because of the word of God and the testimony they had maintained. They called out in a loud voice, 'How long, Sovereign Lord, holy and true, until you judge the inhabitants of the earth and revenge our blood?' Then each of them was given a white robe, and they were told to wait a while longer, until the number of their fellow servants and brothers who were to be killed as they had been was completed." Revelation 20:4 adds this to their number, "I saw thrones on which were seated those who had been given authority to judge. And I saw the souls of those who had been beheaded because of their testimony for Jesus and because of the word of God. They had not worshipped the beast or his image and had not received the mark of the beast on their foreheads or on their hands. They came to life and reigned with Christ a thousand years."

As this book has been relating these future events, it should be clearing up for the reader what the future holds and some of the current events that are laying a foundation for it, and thus contributing to its fulfillment. The question then begging to be answered is this: "What are we as Christians to be doing as we occupy this time and space?" The answer to that question is this: First, we are to be praying. Secondly, we are to be wielding our authority in Christ against evil and the evil one! And thirdly, we are to be alert and be aware of the steps being taken to initiate a socialistic world government so that we can vote and lift our voices against it. Finally, we are to share what is happening on earth with those around us.

If Satan has his way, the world will come to an end with the nations being totally deceived about the role they are to be playing in the globalization effort. They will be deceived into believing that it is necessary for them to travel to Israel to destroy the Jewish people because they are obstructing efforts to unify the world religiously and politically. The church, before it is taken out of the milieu, has its marching orders from the Commander-in-chief. Remember back to the conversation God had with Satan recorded fictitiously, but deductively, earlier in this book. Satan wanted God to allow him to reign over all the people who would eventually live on the face of this earth. He reassured God that he would deflect to him the worship the people on this world would give to him. When

God said no to all of the attempts of Satan to gain this position, Satan asked God to allow man to choose whom they wanted to be god. In the discussion, Satan received the assurance from God that if he were successful, that God would not destroy Adam and Eve and start over with a new couple with whom he would populate the earth. The two also agreed that they would not superimpose their will on mankind, but would work with people to accomplish their two very different goals. God has abided by this agreement throughout history. The Old Testament records the decision God made in choosing Abraham and his descendents to represent him to the world in which they lived. By their own free will they chose to obey God and follow his directives. From that same Jewish community he chose special prophets to record all his correspondence with them. One of the most important communications God gave to them was given to Abraham. He was told by God, "Leave your country, your people and your father's household and go to the land I will show you. I will make you into a great nation and I will bless you; I will make you name great and you will be a blessing. I will bless those who bless you, and whoever curses you I will curse; and all peoples on the earth will be blessed through you." (Genesis 12:1-3) God was announcing to Abraham his plan to bring Salvation to the world. The Apostle Paul understood this when he wrote to the Christians in Galatia, "Consider Abraham. He believed God and it was reckoned to him as righteousness. Understand, then, that those who believe are children of Abraham. The Scripture foresaw that God would justify the Gentiles by faith, and announced the Gospel in advance to Abraham: 'All the nations will be blessed through you.' So those who have faith are blessed along with Abraham, the man of faith." (Galatians 3:6-7)

In the New Testament, God has placed every believer in the church, which is the embodiment of the Lord Jesus Christ. The church is to radiate the presence and work of God amongst its members. Ephesians, the greatest epistle about the church, was written by the Apostle Paul. In it he writes, "For this reason, ever since I heard of your faith in the Lord Jesus Christ, and love for all the saints, I have not stopped giving thanks for you, remembering you in my prayers. I keep asking that the God of our Lord Jesus Christ, the Father of glory, may give unto you the Spirit of wisdom and revelation, so that you may know him better. I pray also that the eyes of your heart may be enlightened in order that you may know the hope to which he has called you, the riches of his glorious inheritance in the saints, and his incomparably great power for us who believe. That power is like the working of his mighty strength, which he exerted in Christ when he raised him from the dead and seated him at his right hand in heavenly realms, far above all rule and authority, power and dominion, and every title that can be given, not only in this present age, but also in the one to come. And God placed all things under his feet and appointed him to be head over everything for the church, which is his body, the fullness of him who fills everything in every way."

The church is the vehicle by which God has chosen to make himself visible to this world. In the same way God chose Israel to make himself known, he now has chosen the church to do the same thing. God has equipped the church to successfully fulfill his purpose by giving gifts to the church. Ephesians 4:11 states that after Jesus fulfilled his mission here on earth, he went back to heaven. Before he left, he gave the church Apostles, prophets, evangelists and pastors and teachers. The Word of God necessary to transfer people out of the kingdom of darkness into the kingdom of God's dear Son, was given to the Apostles and prophets. To share the Good News of the Gospel recorded in God's Word, God gave evangelists. And to use the Word of God to build up those who had become believers in Jesus Christ as their Lord and Savior, he gave to the church pastors and teachers. Ephesians 4:12 described the goal of these people who are God's gift to the church: "to prepare God's people for works of service, so that the body of Christ may be built up until we all attain to unity in the faith and knowledge of the Son of God and become mature, attaining to the whole measure of the fullness of Christ."

Because the church is to exist in a "fallen world" whose god is Satan, the church can expect resistance from him and his angels who have shown allegiance to him. Therefore God has equipped each Christian with armor with which to do battle against the onslaught of the demons. Ephesians 6:11-18 describes the armor God has given to members of his church body to protect them from the wiles of the devil. "Put on the full armor of God so you can take your stand against the devil's schemes. For our struggle is not against flesh and blood, but against the rulers, against the authorities, against the powers of this dark world and against the spiritual forces of evil in the heavenly realms. Therefore put on the full armor of God, so that when the day of evil comes, you may be able to stand your ground, and after you have done everything, to stand. Stand firm then, with the belt of truth buckled around your waist, with the breastplate of righteousness in place, and with your feet fitted with the readiness that comes from the gospel of peace. In addition to all this, take up the shield of faith with which you can extinguish all the flaming arrows of the evil one. Take the helmet of salvation and the sword of the Spirit, which is the Word of God. And pray in the Spirit on all occasions with all kinds of prayers and requests. With this in mind, be alert and always keep on praying for all the saints."

In this passage of Scripture from Ephesians 6, God has alerted us to the existence of an unseen enemy to those who compose the church. For a fuller discussion of the four categories of evil spirits listed here, read my book, "Looking At The Unseen". Suffice it to write here, Satan has many angels at his disposal who are directed to shoot flaming arrows at Christians. 'Screwtape Letters", a book written by C.S. Lewis, discloses the many forms these arrows take. The first piece of the armor we are to use against Satan's attempts to harm us is truth. The reason we are to use the belt of truth is given in my book, "The Truth About The Lie". Jesus said in John 8:44 while describing Satan that "He was a murderer from the beginning, not holding to the truth, for there is no truth in him. When he lies, he speaks his native language, for he is a liar and the father of it." Satan fathered the lie in the Garden of Eden with Eve when he told her she need not depend on God or what he had said. This is the essence of "the lie" and is contained in every temptation hurled at the Christian. The belt of truth is what the Christian is to use to counter the lie in the temptations they encounter. Truth has the definite article with it. That means there is specific content associated with the word truth. Jesus said he was "the truth." (John 14:6) That means his life reflected "the truth". He said in the Upper Room Discourse that he didn't do anything except what the Father directed him to do and he didn't say anything the Father didn't direct him to say. He depended totally on his Father. An illustration of this fact is seen from the way he prayed. He prayed all night before choosing his disciples. "The truth" characterized the life of Jesus and is to represent how we live our lives as well. So when Satan tempts us with "the lie" that we can do something without praying about it or consulting another Christian for wisdom, we are to pray showing our dependence on God. 1 Corinthians 10:13 instructs the Christian that "there is now no temptation that comes to us that is not common to man, but God is faithful, who will not allow us to be tempted beyond what we are able, but will with the temptation allow a way of escape..." The "common temptation" is "the lie" that is a part of every temptation. The "way of escape" is the truth as exemplified in Jesus who depended on God for everything. This is why we are told to "pray about everything" (Philippians 4:6) which gives us God's peace knowing that he will take care of the thing about which we have asked. Wearing the belt of truth is evidence we know that our adversary and his henchmen are liars and come at us with an arsenal of lies.

The breastplate of righteousness is an essential part of the armor of God because the Devil is the "accuser of the brethren has been thrown down, who accuses them before God night and day." (Revelation 12:10) Of what does he accuse us? The Devil accuses us of not being the children of God. Righteousness refers to having a right standing before God. Satan accuses us of being sinful and shameful bastards, not the true children of God through faith. He tells God we try to please him through our works and thus claim a righteousness of our own based on our own works. Satan had convinced the Jews that the Law given by Moses to the Jewish people was able to justify the Jews before God. The Apostle Paul informed the Jewish leadership "that by the works of the Law no one would be justified." (Romans 3:20) The Apostle Paul painted a different picture of the true Christian in Romans 4. There he argued that the righteousness of Abraham was by faith, not works of the Law. To establish his argument he stated that Abraham was uncircumcised at the time he was declared righteous by God. And since circumcision was a sign of adherence to the Law of Moses, his circumcision came after the fact, and that his faith made him a child of God and put him in right standing before God. Therefore he concluded that "if by the transgression of the one death reigned through the one, much more those who receive the abundance of grace and the gift of righteousness will reign in life through the one, Jesus Christ." (Romans 5:17) And then the Apostle added, "the Law came in that the transgression might increase, but where sin increased, grace abounded all the more, that as sin reigned in death, even so grace might reign through righteousness to eternal life through Jesus Christ our Lord." (Romans 5:20-21) The content of the temptation sent to us by Satan is that more is needed than the work of Jesus Christ to put the Christian in right standing before God. He haunts the Christian with thoughts of guilt and fear that he hasn't done enough to secure eternal life before God. By wearing the breastplate of righteousness, the Christian declares that "by faith we are saved through faith, and not of ourselves, it is the gift of God, not of works, lest any many should boast." (Ephesians 2:8-9) Therefore we as Christians can eliminate false feelings of guilt and fear, knowing that the righteousness we have is imputed by God. (Romans 4:6) Some translations have the word "reckon" instead of "imputed". God has done all the work in Christ Jesus our Lord to secure our relationship as children of God. Say this to Satan when he tries to rob you of your peace with God by the righteousness you wear. Remember what God said about Abel. Hebrews 11:4 states "by faith Abel offered to God a better sacrifice to God than Cain, through which he obtained the testimony that he was righteous, God testifying about his gifts, and through faith, though he is dead, he still speaks." Abel brought the very best animal out of his flock to sacrifice to God. This gift jeopardized the pedigree of future flocks, but Abel believed God would provide and trusted God completely by giving God the very best he had to offer. When you surrender your life to God as part of your worship, it reflects your right standing (righteousness) before God. (Romans 12:1)

The next article of our armor relates to our feet and having been fitted with the proper shoes. The shoes with which we are to wear are the Gospel of Peace. Peace comes from being forgiven by God for all of our sins. The Apostle Paul wrote in Romans 5:1 that "having been justified by faith, we have peace with God through our Lord Jesus Christ." Justification is a legal term that relates to a condition in the Christian's life where there is no offensive act being held by God against the Christian. The reason for this condition is that God has forgiven all of our trespasses and placed them on the cross of Christ. There at the cross those sins have been forgiven. Isaiah the prophet looking forward to Christ's death wrote, "All we like sheep have gone astray, we have turned everyone to his own way, but the Lord laid on him the iniquity of us all." (Isaiah 53:6) This is the Gospel and good news we have to share with those who have no peace as they wrestle with feelings of guilt and

144

condemnation. The judge has rendered his verdict of "not guilty" for those who have placed faith in the work of Jesus Christ on the cross. With this good news, we share it with all of the world. That is where Jesus told us to go when he gave the Great Commission, "Go, therefore, and make disciples of all nations, baptizing them in the name of the Father and the Son and the Holy Spirit, teaching them ot observe all that I have commanded you; and lo, I am with you always, even to the end of the age." (Matthew 28:19-20)

The next item of our armor as Christians to wear is the shield of faith. God describes its purpose as "extinguishing all the flaming arrows of the evil one." (Ephesians 6:16) Do not miss the word "all" in this verse because Satan's attack of believers takes many different forms. No matter how he decides to attack you, your shield of faith will protect you. The shield of faith with which you are equipped as a Christian comes from knowing the Bible. The Bible teaches that "faith comes from hearing the word of God." (Romans 10:17) An example of this occurred when Jesus was tempted by the Devil in the wilderness. On three separate occasions Jesus used the word of God to thwart off the Devil's attacks. The attacks were against his whole person, body, soul and spirit. After being in the wilderness some 40 days, the Devil tempted him to use his power as God to turn stones into bread. Jesus responded to this temptation directed at his body's sense of hunger, "It is written, 'man shall not live by bread alone, but by every word that proceeds from the mouth of God.'" (Matthew 4:4) On a different occasion, the Devil took Jesus to the pinnacle of the temple and told him to throw himself down citing Psalm 91:11-12, "He will give his angels charge over you; and on their hands they will bear you up, lest you strike your foot against a stone." Jesus responded to this temptation against his soul composed of mind, will and emotion. He said, "You shall not tempt the Lord Your God." (Matthew 4:7) The fact that the Devil knew Scripture but incorrectly applied it, should alert the Christian to "study to show themselves workman that needs not to be ashamed, rightly dividing the word of truth." (2 Timothy 2:15) The Devil misapplied the Bible, and so can we if we do not do the study necessary to "rightly divide it." To rightly divide it, use the historical-grammatical method of exegesis promoted by Bernard Ramm. Jesus' will was addressed in this temptation directed at his soul. He chose correctly what to do because he knew God's word and how to rightly apply it, which is wisdom.

The final temptation directed at Jesus by the Devil is directed towards his Spirit. The devil offered him a way to avoid the pain and shame of the cross by worshipping him. He said to Jesus after showing him all the nations of the world that he would allow Jesus to govern them if he would bow down and worship him. Jesus' answer to the Devil is recorded in Matthew 4:9, "Be gone, Satan! For it is written, 'You shall worship the Lord Your God, and serve him only.'" Our spirit bears the Image of God as a result of God creating us. He designed the spirit in man to be one with God and thus fulfilled in that relationship with him. Satan's temptation against our spirit is designed for us to value something more than that relationship. Satan offered Jesus the world government. In essence he said this will be your basis of value. You can be known as the head of government and rule under my authority as god. In the same way the Devil's temptation towards us is to offer us a basis of value far removed from our identity as a Christ follower. It could be the country club to which we belong. It could be your social status in the community in which you live. It could be the car you drive or home in which you live that you use as your basis of worth. If this is true then you have bowed your knee to Satan and succumbed to his temptation. Jesus asked this question: "What does it profit a man if he gain the whole world and forfeits his own soul?" The Apostle Paul emphasized this same truth when he wrote, "For the love of Christ controls us, having concluded this, that one died for all, therefore all died; and he died for all, that they who live should no longer live for themselves, but for him who died and rose again on our behalf. Therefore from now on we recognize no man according to the flesh; even though we have known Christ according to the flesh, yet now we know him thus no longer." (2 Corinthians 5:14-16) The Devil attacks us in body, soul and spirit. As long as we have the shield of faith, we will prevail against his attacks.

We are also to take the helmet of Salvation as part of the armor supplied by God. When I was in high school, I played football. I wore a helmet as part of my uniform to protect my head. However, I remember a game where it had rained earlier and the field was soggy. I tried to "juke" a player on the other team to escape being hit by him. However, my cleats slipped and I woke up to smelling salts being administered by one of the coaches. Had I not had on that helmet, I might still be seeing stars. The armor described by God has a helmet to protect our head. It is called Salvation. The writer of Hebrews, probably the Apostle Paul, wrote, "How shall we escape if we ignore such a great salvation? This salvation, which was first announced by the Lord, was confirmed to us by those who heard him. God also testified to it by signs, wonders and various miracles, and gifts of the Holy Spirit distributed according to his will." (Hebrews 2:3-4) Salvation describes from what we are saved. First, we are saved from the penalty of sin called justification. The Aorist tense in the Greek language is used to describe this act in the past, the effects which continue endlessly. Secondly, we are saved from the power of sin called sanctification. Romans Chapters 6-8 address how daily the power of God removes the position of the old nature in our lives as Christians and allows the Spirit of God to instead control our lives. In 2 Corinthians 3 it is called the New Covenant where God is allowed to live the Christian life for us. Finally, we will be saved from the presence of sin called glorification. This will occur at the rapture of the church as addressed in First Thessalonians 4:13-18. This event will remove the church from the world, leaving the nation of Israel to stand against Satan's attempts to annihilate her. (Revelation 12) Finally, Jesus will return and establish his kingdom when the Jewish people repent and call Jesus back to be their long awaited Messiah.

The Bible, the word of God, is also a piece of the armament given to the Christian. It is the offensive weapon to be used by the soldier of Jesus Christ in his battle against Satan. It is to be used as Jesus used it during his temptations. James 4:7 encourages the Christ follower with these words, "Submit to God, resist the devil, and he will flee from you." In other words, "take up your cross daily and follow him" which is submitting to God, then use the word of God to ward off Satan's temptations, and he will flee from you.

The final thing we are to do in our battles with Satan and his fallen host is to pray! "And pray in the Spirit on all occasions with all kinds of prayers and requests." (Ephesians 6:18) Prayer is also an offensive weapon to use in our battle against Satan and his fallen angels. Recall in Luke 10:17 when the seventy two, whom Jesus had sent out in his name, returned. They exclaimed to Jesus that "even the demons are subject to us in your name." Jesus responded to them and said, "I saw Satan fall like lightning from heaven. I have given you authority to trample on snakes and scorpions and to overcome all the power of the enemy, nothing will harm you." Some years ago I was asked to speak on the subject of demonology at our church's National convention. Some months later this prompted a fellow pastor in a nearby community to call me and ask if he could bring a coven leader to me. The person in question was bound by an evil spirit and could not vocalize the name of Jesus. After addressing the evil spirit, and after getting him to admit his defeat when Christ died for the sins of mankind, and for this person, he was forced in the name of Jesus to leave this person. I made it clear to the demon when he left that person, he was not to harm this person in any way. After the demon left, the person was able to name Jesus Christ as Lord and Savior. I told this person to get rid of all the Satanic paraphernalia that had been used in Satanic worship.

Every Christian needs to know that "in Christ" they are raised with him and seated in heavenly places, far above all rule authority, and every name that can be named. From that vantage point we have the permission from Christ to speak and act in his name. Recall the agreement Jesus has with Satan where both agreed to use human beings to accomplish their will. Jesus' will on earth can be done just as it is in heaven by Christians praying. Jesus wants to use you as he did the disciples, to accomplish his will. In this book, I have been explaining Satan's desire to remain god of this world. He is working to deceive peoples and nations in preparation for that final event when he plans to destroy the Jewish people, the only nation that can call Jesus back to this earth and take away his position. The growth of Anti-Semitism in Europe and America is evidence of his work. Globalization projects underway here in America and abroad also evidence his work and are seeded with anti-Jewish rhetoric. He is trying to unite the nations under one leadership called the beast in Revelation. Once that world government exists, the Anti-Christ will rule and all of Satan's desires will be demanded of those he rules. When I listen to the news on Fox Network and see evidence of the work of Satan in the deaths, anarchy and attempts to elimi-nate the voices of reason from Christians and Republicans, I pray specifically that Jesus will throw into hell those demons causing their deception. We have that power "in Christ" and all we need to eliminate the demons is their location and work. Then we can ask specifically for God to intervene. God will do the rest. Jesus said all we had to do was to ask anything in his name and he would do it. (John 14:14) When teaching about the relationship between the vine and the branches in John 15:7, Jesus said, "If you abide in me and my word abides in you, ask whatever you will and I will do it for you." The Christian community has the power to wield the sword of God against those who stand against him. Peace on earth is a noble effort but cannot be achieved without the "peace of God which passes all understanding" (Philippians 4:6-7) reigning in the hearts of mankind through Salvation in Jesus Christ. Until that time comes during the Millennium, we as God's soldiers are to take the battle to Satan. Use the mighty weapon of prayer and watch as did Jesus, Satan fall like lightning from heaven.

Questions:

1. Read Isaiah 44:1-7. What is the God of Israel like?

_____

_____

_____

2. Read Deuteronomy 28. What was God's plan for Israel?

_____

_____

_____

3. In the New Testament, who are God's people and how do they acquire that recognition?

_____

_____

_____

4. What provision has God given to the church that it might distinguish itself?

_____

_____

_____

5. What are your favorite pieces of the armor God has given you to fight victoriously?

_____

_____

_____

6. How has your vision of prayer changed as you read this Chapter?

_____

_____

_____

7. What are your thoughts about globalization and the steps America is taking to join that movement?

_____

_____

_____

8. Describe some of your recent temptations directed at you, body, soul and spirit?

_____

_____

_____

9. Upon what did you previously use as your basis of worth. What is it now?

_____

_____

_____

Chapter Twelve

Today, America is at war. No, Congress has not declared war. In fact, they are completely oblivious and unaware of the war being fought against America. But the war is not just against America, it is worldwide. However, America and Israel are the main targets. America is the target of Satan and all his fellow evil angels who want to repay America for all its benevolences toward the world. Where Satan has created civil war and death, America has come to the aid of those countries with care packages, food and clothing and military assistance when requested. Where Satan has created false religions, America has sent missionaries and organized groups to give hope through the message of salvation and the Gospel of peace. America sends money and aid to those areas of the world suffering the effects of weather like hurricanes or tsunamis. Jesus described Satan as having a cruel nature that delights in murder and death. (John 8:44) Where in history over the last few thousand years Satan has worked there has been death, hatred and inhumanity. America has intervened to alleviate the pain and suffering in many of those places in the world suffering because of the work of Satan and his demonic forces. Satan is totally unhappy with those interventions. He wants nothing less than to destroy America and the gospel which has created the desire in people to help other people in need. He hates America for all the good it has done and in the process, thwarted his activity. As long as America keeps sending missionaries and goods for humanitarian needs, Satan will continue his attacks on America.

Instead of focusing on the good America has done for the world, there is a movement in America to focus on its failures, rather than its benevolences. The "Critical race theory" being taught in our schools and even to our Armed Forces, is designed to create hatred and division among Americans. Who is behind that movement and wants to use it to the detriment of our society? It is a part of the package developed by Satan in his war against America. Yes, humans in Europe originally thought up the idea, but who influenced their thinking? In contrast to the "Critical race theory" exists the truth that everyone has been created in the Image of God. Moreover, the Bible teaches when clothed with Christ, "There is neither Jew nor Greek, slave not free, male nor female, for you are all one in Christ Jesus." (Galatians 3:28) In another place in the Bible, it is clearly taught that the results of changed hearts in Christians results in not knowing any man any longer according to the flesh. Christians are to love and care for one another. The Apostle John wrote, "Dear friends, let us love one another, for love comes from God. Everyone who loves has been born of God and knows God. Whoever does not love does not know God, because God is love. This is how God showed his love among us: He sent his only Son into the world that we might live through him. This is love, not that we first loved him, but he loved us and gave us his Son as an atoning sacrifice for our sins." (1 John 4:7-10)

The reason for this warfare ultimately is because Satan has a plan to maintain his position as the god of this fallen world. He desires to bring America to its knees and remove the mantel of leadership it has provided to the world. He is using Democratic leadership in our country to change our country from a democracy into a socialistic dictatorship that silences the voices of the people of America. Twitter and facebook and other groups thwart free speech and remove their employees who blow the whistle on their activity and attempts to expose their policies. The Democrats opened the border of this country to illegal immigrants, excusing themselves by using humanitarian reasons to explain their policies. They offer them to deceive Americans. Rather their goal is to gain the votes of those people to counter the votes of Republicans. They want these illegal immigrants to receive Driver's Licenses which in turn will give them access to voting machines. They want a blue America with the values they have already embraced. They promote abortions and the taking of life even after the baby is born. They promote anarchy by reducing the police forces in our communities. Chicago's mayor Lightfoot has already asked for federal troops. This was her plan all along to turn her city over to national control. She was willing allow thousands of people to be murdered to accomplish her real goal. This attempt to nationalize a police force is to make America dependent on government. It is part of a globalization strategy spearheaded by the liberal "left" in our country.

The "left" promotes lawlessness by allowing felons back onto our streets after they have committed crimes. Jesus said that lawlessness would be a signal to any nation that the end was near. (Matthew 24:12) Judges here in America even applaud those who commit crimes against society. Our Vice President Harris gave money to bail out those arrested in Minneapolis for burning buildings and attacking, and in some cases, killing store owners who were trying to protect their life's dream of owning and operating a business. Women are raped and hit in the face as they walk down the streets of America. Organizations like Black Lives Matter which are internally organized along Marxist ideologies, exist so that the leadership can line their own pockets with the donations intended to alleviate the suffering of black people. In Chicago many black people have died, but BLM members are not there to stop the onslaught. Instead they march chanting about "dead cops and wanting them now." Their true intent is about buying expensive houses for themselves. Antifa is an organization, where behind the scenes can be located Satan, which is committed to the destruction of America. They are attempting to do so my removing anything that reminds America of its history and culture. They want to eliminate the statues of heroes and redact our history to remove evidence of our Christian heritage. They work to remove the names of our past presidents from schools. They want a godless society so they remove the Ten Commandments from our courts. They are like Goliath, who in the history of Israel, was a Philistine who wanted to destroy the nation of Israel and make it a nation subservient to his own country with its godless values. Goliath was a giant of a man, standing nine feet six inches tall. He definitely could dunk a basketball. (My anecdote) When the Philistines drew up battle lines to fight against Israel, Goliath came forward and offered to fight a soldier from the army of Israel under King Saul's command. His offer was to avoid all the bloodshed and carnage of warfare by fighting the representative of Israel in a fight to the finish. The nation of the winning soldier would place into captivity the people of the slain soldier. Those peoples would serve as slaves to the conquering nation, the men working and the women serving as household servants and sexual slaves.

One day David was sent by his father to his three brothers in Israel's army. He brought them some homemade bread and special food not found in the rations given to them in the army. When David heard the proud boasts of Goliath in the name of his false god, Dagon, he was surprised that no soldier went out to battle Goliath in the name of the God of Israel. Finally, King Saul heard of David's presence and his belief in Israel's God who would give Israel the victory. David gave Saul his resume of killing the lions and bears that came to eat his flock of sheep while he shepherded them. Saul gave David permission to go out and battle Goliath. As David approached the giant of a man, Goliath, Goliath said to him, "Am I a dog that you come at me with sticks? I will give your flesh to the birds of the air and the beasts of the field." (1 Samuel 17:44) David replied with these words, "You come against me with sword and spear and javelin, but I come against you in the name of the Lord Almighty, the God of the armies of Israel, whom you have defied. This day the Lord will hand you over to me and I will strike you down and cut off your head." (1 Samuel 17:45-47) The Bible says that Goliath moved toward David, yet David ran at the giant. He gathered five rocks from a brook and went out to meet Israel's adversary. He took five rocks since Goliath had 4 brothers. David put a rock into his sling and let it fly. When I was growing up there was a saying about Superman that he could fly faster than a speeding bullet. This stone flew at least that fast. A bullet flies usually at a speed of about 1130 feet/second. It can penetrate the skull of human being which in this case it did. The Bible says this stone "sank into the forehead of Goliath and he died. As he fell, his last words were, "Nothing like that ever entered my mind before!" (Again, my anecdote) Just as David had the assurance that God would give him the victory over Goliath, so every Christian can have that same assurance when they pray. God has said, "Greater is he that is in you than he that is in the world." (1 John 4:4) Ephesians 3:20 teaches the Christians that "he cannot even ask or think of the things God is able to do for them and through them, according to the power that works within them." The Apostle Paul is referring to the Holy Spirit that every Christian has resident within them. Therefore do not flinch at the adversary who comes to do battle with you. No matter what form he takes, run at him equipped to win the battle. It is said many times throughout the Bible, "the battle is not yours, it belongs to the Lord God Almighty'." Therefore, let's stand against our real foe, not flesh and blood, but...the Devil. (Ephesians 6) We have nothing to worry about. Six times in the Sermon on the Mount recorded in Matthew 6, God said "not to worry." The Living Bible translates Philippians 4:6-7 with these words: "Worry about nothing, but pray about everything, and the

157

peace of God which passes all understanding shall stand guard over your emotions." Sometimes the News broadcasts paint a very unsettling picture of the dilemma America faces. What are we to do? The answer to that question is, don't worry, but pray. You have a God infinite in power who is waiting to hear from you in prayer so that he can unleash his power. Then "God's will will be done on earth as it is in heaven." However, scripture states that "we have not because we ask not." (James 4:2) Let us begin asking since Jesus said, "Ask me anything and I will do it!" Jesus also said if two men agree about anything, they can ask God and "it shall be done for them by my Father who is in heaven." (Matthew 18:19) Though this verse addresses a specific situation, it can also be applied to the will of God being done.

This mayhem in our world has an orchestra leader. Wherever there is lawlessness and crime, Satan and his fallen angels are cheerleaders. The way to force him to flee is given in the following formula: "Submit to God, resist Satan, and he will flee from you." (James 4:7) Submitting to God means to surrender your life to the will of God. His will for you is to be Holy as He is Holy. Initially, God gave the Ten Commandments for his people to follow if they wanted to be Holy. Those Ten Commandments, among other things, calls for the cessation of killing and crime and the hurting of others. The first five of those commandments describes how to adhere to the last five. They are listed as follows from Exodus 20:2-25: "1. Have only God as your God; 2. Have no images of God; 3. Do not use the Lord's name is vain; 4. Remember God on the Sabbath; 5. Honor you father and mother; 6. You shall not murder; 7. You shall not commit adultery; 8. You shall not steal; 9. You shall not lie; 10. You shall not covet anything belonging to another person." Jesus summarized the first five commandments by verbalizing the greatest of all the commandments, recorded in Matthew 22:37, "Love the Lord your God with all your heart and with all your soul and with all your mind. This is the first and greatest commandment." Then, Jesus proceeded to summarize the final 5 commandments with these words, "And the second is like it, 'Love your neighbor as yourself.'" (Matthew 22:39) If you truly love your neighbor as a Christian, you will want to give to him, not take his life, or wife, or possessions or reputation or anything else he may own or possess. To get Satan to flee it is first necessary to "submit to God". In the words of the greatest of all commandments it is to "love the Lord your God with all your heart, soul and mind."

To fill your heart with love for God requires that you first focus on his love for you. The Bible says "God demonstrated his love for us in that while we were yet sinners, Christ died for us." (Romans 5:8) Look at what Jesus endured to forgive our sins. The prophet Isaiah looked ahead 700 years from when he lived and wrote what he saw, namely the disfigured body of Jesus hanging on the cross. "There were many who were appalled at him --- his appearance was so disfigured beyond that of any man and his form marred beyond human likeness." (Isaiah 52:14) Isaiah continues to explain why the death of Jesus was necessary. He wrote that it was necessary to pay of our sins in Isaiah 53:4-12, "Surely he took up our infirmities and carried our sorrows, yet we considered him stricken by God, smitten by him and afflicted. But he was pierced for our transgressions, he was crushed for our iniquities; the punishment that brought us peace was upon him, and by his wounds we are healed. We all like sheep have gone astray, each of us has turned to his own way; and the Lord has laid on him the iniquity of us all. He was oppressed and afflicted, yet he did not open his mouth, he was led like a lamb to the slaughter and as a sheep before her shearers is silent, so he did not open his mouth. By oppression and judgment he was taken away. And who can speak of his descendents? For he was cut off from the land of the living; for the transgressions of my people he was stricken. He was assigned a grave with the wicked, and with the rich in his death, though he had done no violence, nor was any deceit found in his mouth. Yet it was the Lord's will to crush him and cause him to suffer, and though the Lord makes his life a guilt offering, he will see his suffering and prolong his days, and the will of the Lord will of the Lord will prosper in his hand. After the suffering of his soul, he will see the light of life and be satisfied; by his knowledge my righteous servant will justify many, and he will bear their iniquities. Therefore I will give him a position among the great, and he will divide the spoils with the strong, because he poured out his life unto death, and was numbered with the transgressors. For he bore the sin of many, and made intercession for the transgressor."

This scripture teaches that God saw the work of Christ, and it was enough to satisfy the debt we owed him for our sins and transgressions. In the film "The Passion of Christ," the visualization of what Isaiah the prophet foresaw should cause us all the fall in love with the God who wanted to fellowship with us so badly that he endured the cross for us. When filled with that love in our own hearts, we can love God and others. That transforming love will change how we think about ourselves and others so that we serve one another, as opposed to taking from each other as the prohibitions in the Ten Commandments illustrate. With God's love in our hearts and armed with the Scriptures to resist Satan, he will flee from us. This is the only formula that is going to save America and the church of Jesus Christ from Satan's attacks.

Therefore, my fellow Christian soldier, let's be alert. Let us be confident knowing the same power that raised Christ from the grave is resident in our lives and is available to us to use against the schemes and wiles of the Devil. (Ephesians 3:20-21; Philippians 3) When one listens to the News channels, one can be consumed with fear at what the Democrats have accomplished and are able to do because they control both houses of government, the press and many judges who sit on the benches of our courts. However, listen to the plight of an Old Testament King who had one of the strongest alliances of nations (32 kings) gathered against him and Israel.

At his doorstep was Ben-Hadad, King of Aram. (1 Kings 20) God had warned King Ahab that the Syrians would be attacking and so King Ahab was prepared to battle them. King Ahab won the battle, but spared Ban-Hadad's life against the wishes of God. The Syrians had been defeated earlier by King Ahab in the mountains, so the Syrians chose to wage war on the plains, conceding that Israel's God was God of the hills. Once King Ahab defeated Syria again, they now believed the God of Israel was the God of the hills and the plains. Ben-Hadad had a son, Ben-Hadad ll. Even though the prophet Elisha healed his commander-in-chief, Naaman, of leprosy, Ben-Hadad ll sent his armies to arrest Elisha since he was informing King Ahab on the whereabouts of his army. This enabled the army of Israel to avoid a battle that might lead to their capture and defeat. When the army of Ben-Hadad ll arrived, the Prophet of God, Elisha, smote that army with blindness before sending them back to their King. (2 Kings 6:8-23) Ben-Hadad ll later sent his army to lay siege against Samaria. Families were eating the flesh of family members who died, so great was the ensuing famine and hunger caused by the siege. Some hungry outcasts suffering from leprosy had to inform the armies of Israel what God had done on their behalf. Again God intervened and Ben-Hadad ll''s army abandoned their siege and ran leaving all their food and belongings in their camp. They thought the kings of Musri and the northern Hittites were mounting a surprise attack. Again God showed the peoples and armies around Israel that the God of Israel would be true to his promises of protecting his people. (Deuteronomy 28) Ben-Hadad ll had to learn that lesson the hard way that God was going to protect the people through whom he would bring the Messiah into the world.

In the same way, God has promised never to leave you or forsake you. Like he did for the Old Testament figure, Job, God will do for you. God has promised to put a hedge around you like he did Job. (Job 1:10) Though Satan accused God of blessing Job and thus soliciting his allegiance, God allowed Satan to take away some of those blessings to prove him wrong. Satan said Job would curse God instead of worshipping him once the blessings were removed. Job's response to this testing was worship when he said, "Naked I came from my mother's womb, and naked I will depart. The Lord gave and the Lord has taken away; May the name of the Lord be praised." (Job 1:29-21) What Job in essence was saying is this: the experience of knowing God personally and intimately as I do is thousands of times better than having a family, wealth and health. Are you able to say this same thing as a result of your relationship with God? Earlier in this Chapter I related Biblical evidence of God's faithfulness to his people. In the same way he will give you the spiritual strength necessary to prevail against Satan and his wiles. Therefore where you see him working, stand up against the strongholds he is attempting to build. "For though we live in the world, we do not wage war as the world does. The weapons we fight with are not the weapons of the world. On the contrary, they have divine power to demolish strongholds. We demolish arguments and every pretension that sets itself up against the knowledge of God, and we take captive every thought to make it obedient to Christ." (2 Corinthians 10:3-5) As we take up the fight against Satan, remember what God has said, "My God shall supply all your needs according to his riches in glory." (Philippians 4:19)

Questions:

1. What are the weapons of our warfare against Satan mentioned in 2 Corinthians 10?

2. "Rice Christians" is a term used to describe people who say they are Christians only to receive the gifts the missionaries give them. This is what Satan accused Job of being! Why was this not true for him? Why is it not true for you?

3. What lessons were you taught in the Biblical accounts about Ben-Hadad ll?

4. Explain why the first five commandments in the Ten Commandments together form the greatest of the Commandments?

5. How can "defund the police" slogans and practices within city governments be reconciled with God giving the Ten Commandments?

_____

_____

_____

6. Read Isaiah 52-53. What cost was God willing to pay to forgive our sins and fellowship with us?

_____

_____

_____

7. If you have ever watched the movie, <u>The Passion of Christ</u>, then describe your feelings as you watched Jesus being flogged.

_____

_____

_____

8. Have you enlisted in the war being fought against America, our churches, and your fellow believers?

_____

_____

_____

Chapter Thirteen

"What on earth is happening?" is the question posed by this book. What is happening now is all designed to culminate in the future events recorded in Revelation 19. The one exception to that is that Satan believes the results of the final battle are far different than the one written on the pages of Scripture. He does not believe Jesus Christ will return as the King of Kings and Lord of Lords and fight the final battle against the nations of the world assembled against him. The reason he believes Jesus will not return is because Jesus promised to not return until the Jewish people called him back to be their Messiah. Jesus is quoted as saying, "O Jerusalem, Jerusalem, who kills the prophets and stones those sent to her! How often I wanted to gather your children together, the way a hen gathers her chicks under her wings, and you were unwilling. Behold, your house is being left to you desolate. For I say unto you, from now on you shall not see me until you say, 'Blessed is he who comes in the name of the Lord.'" (Matthew 23:37-39) Therefore, according to Scripture, before Jesus returns as the Jewish Messiah, the Jewish people must call him back as such. They are to do so by repenting of their national sin of rejecting the Messiah and then plead for his return. The words by which they will do this are recorded in Hosea 5:15-6:3, "I will go away (Jesus speaking) and return to my place until they acknowledge their guilt and seek my face; in their affliction they will earnestly seek me saying, 'Come let us return to the Lord. For he has torn us, but he will heal us; He has wounded us,, but he will bandage us. He will revive us after two days; he will raise us up on the third day that we may live before him. So let us know, let us press on to know the Lord. His going forth is as certain as the dawn; and he will come to us like rain, like the spring rain watering the earth.'" The word "saying" at the end of Hosea 5 is in the original text but is omitted from your translation of the Bible. The word "guilt" in Hosea 5:15 refers to the Jewish rejection of Jesus as their Messiah. They will confess their national sin and rejection of the truth as recorded in Isaiah 53:1-9.

Satan doesn't believe this repentance by the Jewish people will happen because, according to his plan, at the end of the age there will be no Jewish people alive on this planet to call Jesus back to be their Messiah. Jesus taught that Satan's plan would have been successful except for Jesus' intervention. Jesus said, "And unless those days had been cut short, no life would have been saved, but for the sake of the elect those days shall be cut short." (Matthew 24:22) Who are the elect? The Apostle Paul answers that question in Romans 8:33-34, "Who shall bring a charge against God's elect? God is the one who justifies; who is the one who condemns? Jesus Christ is He who died, yes, rather who was raised, who is at the right hand of God, who intercedes for us." According to this text, the elect are those whom God has justified. Romans 5:1-2 describes the "justified" as follows: "Therefore having been justified by faith, we have peace with God through our Lord Jesus Christ, through whom also we have obtained our introduction by faith into this grace in which we stand, and we exult in hope of the glory of God." If we have been to the foot of the cross and there repented of our sin, and placed faith in his work there to forgive us of our sins, God justifies us. We are then the "elect". The "elect" are born-again Christians.

One may then ask, who are the elect at the time described by Jesus' words recorded in Matthew 24:22? Was Jesus using the term differently than the Apostle Paul in Romans 8:33-34? Wasn't the Apostle Paul writing about Christians in Romans 8? How does that Scripture apply if there are no more Christians on earth after the Church has been raptured? Jesus' words in Matthew 24:22 are referring to a time when he returns to earth to save the Jewish people from being annihilated by the armies of the earth under the direction of the Anti-Christ. The Bible refers to this event as the time of Jacob's trouble in Jeremiah 30:7-9. "Alas! For that day is great. There is none like it. And it is the time of Jacob's trouble. But he will be saved through it. 'And it shall come about in that day', declares the Lord of hosts, 'that I will break his yoke from off their neck, and will tear off their bonds from their neck and strangers will no longer make them their slaves. But they will serve the Lord their God, and David their king, whom I will raise up for them.'" These days will be filled with great tribulation so that God says about them, "There is none like it!" It is easy to agree with that statement after reading about what transpires in those days recorded in Revelation 11-19. When the church at Thessalonica was experiencing great distress for a time, they thought their trouble was due to the fact that "The Day of The Lord" had come and they missed it. In this sense they were Post-tribulationists. The Apostle Paul wrote 2 Thessalonians to them to clear up their error in holding to that position. He reminded them that a couple of things would proceed the "Day of the Lord" which they thought they had missed. In 2 Thessalonians 2:3-12, The Apostle Paul gave this instruction, "Let no one in any way deceive you, for it will not come unless the apostasy comes first, and the man of lawlessness is revealed, the son of destruction, who opposes and exalts himself above every so-called god or object of worship, so that he takes his seat in the temple of God, displaying himself as being god. Do you not remember that while I was still with you, I was telling you these things? And you know what restrains him now, so that in his time he may be revealed. For the mystery of lawlessness is already at work; only he who now restrains will do so until he is taken out of the way. And then the lawless one will be revealed whom the Lord will slay with the breath of his mouth and bring to an end by the appearance of his coming; that is, the one whose coming is in accord with the activity of Satan with all power and signs and wonders, and with all the deception of wickedness for those who perish, because they did not receive the love of the truth so as to be saved. And for this reason God will send upon them a deluding influence so that they might believe the lie, in order that they all may be judged who did not believe the truth, but took pleasure in wickedness."

The phrase "those days" uttered by Jesus is a reference to the events and time described in Revelation 19:11-21, "And I saw heaven opened, and behold a white horse, and he who sat upon it is called Faithful and True; and in righteousness He judges and wages war. And his eyes are a flame of fire, and upon his head are many diadems and he has a name written upon him which no one knows except himself. And He is clothed with a robe dipped in blood, and his name is called The Word of God. And the armies which are in heaven, clothed in fine linen, white and clean, were following him on white horses. And from his mouth comes a sharp sword, so that with it Ne might smite the nations, and He will rule them with a rod of iron; and He treads the wine press of the fierce wrath of God, the Almighty. And on his robe and on his thigh He has written, King of Kings and Lord of Lords. And I saw the beast and the kings of the earth, and their armies, assembled to make war against Him who sits upon the horse, and against his army. And the beast was seized, and with him the false prophet who performed the signs in his presence, by which he deceived those who had received the mark of the beast and those who worshipped his image; these two were thrown alive into the lake of fire which burns with brimstone. And the rest were killed with the sword which came from the mouth of him who sat upon the horse, and all the birds were filled with their flesh."

The events enumerated in the last Chapters of Revelation, according to Hosea 5, are designed to bring Israel to its knees in repentance. Prior to that the church will have been raptured (1 Thessalonians 4:14-18) and the saints will sit in heaven waiting for Jesus' Second Coming. Other believers killed after the Abomination of Desolation (Daniel 9:24-27) are also there in heaven and ask the Lord how long it will be before he avenges their death. (Revelation 6:9) The Bible teaches the dead to be an enumerable group made up of Jews and Gentiles. In Revelation 7:9-17 we read, "After these things I looked, and behold, a great multitude, which no one could count, from every nation and all tribes and peoples and tongues, standing before the throne and before the Lamb, clothed in white robes, and palm branches were in their hands; and they cry out in a loud voice, saying, 'Salvation to our God who sits on the throne and to the Lamb.' And all the angels were standing around the throne, and around the elders and the four living creatures; and they fell on their faces before the throne and worshiped God, saying, 'Amen, blessing and glory and wisdom and thanksgiving and honor and power and might, be our God forever and ever, Amen.'

The Lord Jesus announced in Matthew 24:14 that "the gospel of the kingdom shall be preached in the whole world for a witness to all the nations, and then the end shall come." The "great multitude" described in Revelation 7:9 is the result of the gospel being preached in the whole world. The logical question is who did the preaching of the Gospel? The answer is discovered in Revelation 11:7-13. During the first three and one-half years of the Seventieth Week of Daniel God appointed two witnesses to "prophecy" to the people in Jerusalem and via television, to the whole world. God protected them during the assigned time they were to minister. If people tried to kill them, fire would proceed out of their mouth and kill their enemies. From what they were able to do seemed to parallel their activity when they lived on the earth. They were able to smite the earth with plague, drought, fire and famine; they could turn the water blood red. Who did those things in Israel's history but Moses and Elijah. Remember the word of God in Malachi 4:5 where God says "Behold, I am going to send you Elijah the prophet before the coming of the great and terrible day of the Lord." Elijah came with Moses and preached the gospel. After their ministry was complete, "the beast will make war with them and kill them. Their bodies will lie in the street for three and one-half days while the earth parties and celebrates their death. Then after three and one-half days, God will say to them, "Come up here." (Revelation 11:12) After they ascend to heaven, there is going to be a great earthquake, "and a tenth of the city fell, and seven thousand people were killed in the earthquake, and the rest were terrified and gave glory to the God of heaven." (Revelation 11:13) The idiom "gave glory to the God of heaven" means the people there who witnessed this became Christians. They are the 144,000 mentioned in Revelation 7 and 14. After they were sealed with the name of the Lamb's father on their forehead, they went and evangelized the world. (Revelation 14:1) Those that believed became the "elect" God would redeem. These events will happen midst great persecution authored by the Anti-Christ. Here is what God said about those who died because of their faith in Jesus Christ during this period, "Here is the perseverance of the saints who keep the commandments of God and their faith in Jesus. And I heard a voice from heaven, saying, 'Write, Blessed are the dead who die in the Lord from now on!' 'Yes,' says the Spirit, 'that they may rest from their labors, for their deeds follow with them.'" (Revelation 14:12-13)

When Jesus returns at the request of the Jewish people, he returns to save the "elect" who are Jewish Christians who have placed faith in Jesus Christ as their savior and Messiah. They did so as a result of the preaching of the 144,000. According to Zachariah 13:8-9, The Bible predicts that "'It will come about in all the land,'" declares the Lord, 'that two parts in it will be cut off and perish; but the third will be left in it. And I will bring the third part through the fire, refine them as silver is refined, and test them as gold is tested. Then they will call on my name, and I will answer them. I will say, 'They are my people,' and they will say, 'The Lord is my God.'" The prophet Zachariah looked into the future and saw the Lord's return. He saw that when he returned he saved one third of the Jewish people. (Zachariah 13:8-9) The people he saved were those who fled Jerusalem and Judea when the Abomination of Desolation occurred in Jerusalem. (Matthew 24:15) For Jesus said that this event would mark the beginning of the greatest persecution in the history of the world. (Matthew 24:21) This persecution would be directed at the Jewish people according to Revelation 12. And the author of this persecution is the Devil, for the reason stated earlier in this book. He wants to destroy every Jew so that they cannot call Jesus Christ back to this earth as their Messiah. If Jesus returns, Satan knows his position as god will be terminated and all the prophecies about his demise will be fulfilled. Therefore he goes to work to hinder God from his return. We are informed about that attempt in Revelation 12:1ff. "And a great sign appeared in heaven; a woman clothed with the sun, and the moon under her feet, and on her head a crown of twelve stars. And she was with child; and she cried out, being in labor and in pain to give birth. And another sign appeared in heaven; and behold, a great red dragon having seven heads and ten horns, and on his heads were seven diadems. And his tail swept a third of the stars in heaven, and threw them to the earth. And the dragon stood before the woman who was about to give birth, so that when she gave birth be might devour her child. And she gave birth to a son, a male child, who is to rule all the nations with a rod of iron; and her child was caught up to God and to his throne. And the woman fled into the wilderness where she had a place prepared for her by God, so that there she might be nourished for one thousand two hundred sixty days. (The last 31/2 years of Daniel's 70th week, also called the great tribulation) And there was war in heaven, Michael and his angels waging war against the dragon. And the dragon and his angels waged war, and they were not strong enough, and there was no longer a place for them in heaven. And the great dragon was thrown down, the serpent of old who is called the Devil and Satan, who deceives the whole world; he was thrown down to the earth and his angels were thrown down with him. And I heard a loud voice in heaven saying, 'Now the salvation, and the power, and the kingdom of our God and the authority of his Christ have come, for the accuser of our brothers has been thrown down, who accuses them before God night and day. And they overcame him because of the blood of the Lamb and because of the word of their testimony, and they did not love their life even unto death. For this reason, rejoice, O heavens, and you who dwell in them. Woe to the earth and the sea, because the devil has come down to you, having great wrath, knowing he has only a short time. And when the dragon saw that he had been thrown down to the earth, he persecuted the woman who gave birth to the male child. And the two wings of the great eagle were given to the woman, in order that she might fly into the wilderness to her place, where she might be nourished for a time and times and half a time, from the presence of the serpent. And the serpent poured water like a river out of his mouth after the woman, so that he might cause her to be swept away with the flood. And the earth helped the woman, and the earth opened its mouth and drank up the water which the dragon poured out of his mouth." Remember what God did to Korah and those opposing his leadership through Moses and Aaron, "Then it came about as he finished speaking all these words, that the ground that was under them split open; and the earth opened its mouth and swallowed them up, and their households, and all the men who belonged to

Korah, with their possessions. So they and all that belonged to them went down to Sheol; and the earth closed over them, and they perished from the midst of the assembly." (Numbers 16:31-33) What God did in the Old Testament in causing the earth to split apart, he will do again when Satan tries to send a flash flood after this remnant of Israel. This intervention by God will anger Satan, as the text says, "the dragon was enraged with the woman, and went off to make war with the rest of her offspring, who keep the commandments of God and hold to the testimony of Jesus." Recall the reference to eagle's wings that relate back to Exodus 19:4 where Moses addressed Israel with these words from God, "You yourselves have seen what I did to the Egyptians, and how I bore you up on eagle's wings and brought you to myself." God will protect Israel as he had done in the past history of Israel. The reference to "time and times and half a time" is an idiom for three and one-half years. That is the duration of the last three and one-half years of Daniel's seventieth week prophecy. (Daniel 9:24-27)

When Jesus returns, he will return to Bozrah (Isaiah 63) where he will attack the armies of the world that have assembled in the Valley of Megiddo and marched to Bozrah. The Battle of the Great Day of God Almighty then ensues and Jesus kills those armies all the way back from Bozrah to Jerusalem. (Revelation 16:10-21) The Bible says the blood from that battle runs to a depth from the "horse's bridle (6 feeet) for a distance of 180 miles. (Revelation 14:20) The prophet Joel looked ahead at this time period and wrote on behalf of God, "For behold, in those days and at that time; When I restore the fortunes of Judah and Jerusalem, I will gather all the nations, and bring them down to the valley of Jehoshaphat. Then I will enter into my judgment with them there on behalf of my people and my inheritance, Israel, whom they have scattered among the nations; and they have divided up my land. They have cast lots for my people, traded a boy for a harlot, and sold a girl for wine that they may drink. Moreover, what are you to me, O Tyre, Sidon, and the regions of Philistia? Are you rendering me a recompence? But if you do recompense me, swiftly and speedily I will return your recompense on your head. Since you have taken my silver and gold, brought my precious treasures to your temples, and sold the sons of Judah and Jerusalem to the Greeks in order to remove them far from their territory, behold, I am going to arouse them from the place where you have sold them, and return your recompense on your head...Proclaim this among the nations; Prepare a war; rouse the mighty men! Let all the soldiers draw near, let them come up! Beat your plows into swords, and your pruning hooks into spears; Let the weak say, 'I am a mighty man.' Hasten and come, all you surrounding nations, and gather yourselves there. Bring down, O Lord, they mighty ones. Let the nations be aroused and come up to the valley of Jehoshaphat, for there I will sit to judge all the surrounding nations. Put is the sickle, for the harvest is ripe; Come tread, for the wine press is full. The vats overflow, for their wickedness is great. Multitudes, multitudes in the valley of decision! For the day of the Lord is near in the valley of God's verdict. The sun and the moon grow dark, and the stars lose their brightness. And the Lord roars from Zion and utters his voice from Jerusalem. And the heavens and the earth tremble. But the Lord is a refuge for his people and a stronghold to the sons of Israel. Then you will know that I am the Lord your God, dwelling in Zion my holy mountain. So Jerusalem will be holy, and strangers will pass through it no more." (Joel 3:1-17)

It is clear from these prophetic Scriptures that God has a plan to save Israel from all that Satan has planned to destroy her. At the time of the Abomination of Desolation when temple sacrifice will be forced to stop in Jerusalem, when the Anti-Christ will set up an image of himself in the Holy of Holies in the temple at Jerusalem, when everyone is forced to worship the beast and wear the number with three sets of six numbers on their forehead or wrist, when a world religion will be inaugurated to bring world peace, when a world government will be the fulfillment of a glo-balization Marxist effort, it is clear that many who resist will be killed. It will be easy for the one world government under the control of the beast to persuade constituents of this government to kill Christians and Jews. This globalized Marxist government will have the backing of the one world religious system headed by the false prophet who does miraculous signs as predicted by the Lord Jesus Christ. (Matthew 24:24) This religious system will be headed by members of Islam and the Eastern religions of the world. The Eastern religions teach reincarnation and will use this teaching to persuade people that it is O.K. to murder Christians and Jews. Both Christians and Jews believe their religion is a revealed religion. As such, they believe God is the final authority of truth and practice. They will resist and not be a part of the one world religion. Proponents of the one world religion will teach that having a one world religion is the only way to have world peace. In addition, they will teach that Christians and Jews are against world peace and therefore need to be removed. They will teach that their resistance is due to false teaching in their past. This, they will teach, has led to the deception responsible for their resistance. The only way to cure them is to kill them. Then when they return through the process of reincarnation, they will see the light and support the one world religion and the Marxist government called the beast. Support for this statement comes from Revelation 13:11 "And I saw another beast coming up out of the earth; and he had two horns like a lamb, and he spoke as a dragon. And he exercises all the authority of the first beast in his presence. And he makes the earth and those who dwell in it to worship the first beast, whose fatal wound was healed. And he performs great signs, so that he even makes fire come down out of heaven to the earth in the presence of men. And he deceives those who dwell on the earth because of the signs which it was given him to perform in the presence of the beast, telling those who dwell on the earth to make an image to the beast who had the wound of the sword and has come to life. And there was given to him to him to give breath to the image of the beast, that the image of the beast might even speak and cause as many as do not worship the image of the beast to be killed."

This teaching by the one world religion will support the government's efforts to kill all dissenters to the beast and false prophet. Since everyone wants world peace, and this new religion teaches it has the formula for it, everyone will follow its doctrinal teaching as the only means to achieve it. Since the Jews will not support this one world religion, they will be hated for causing the lack of peace in the world. Thus, everyone on earth will be on board in support of this ethnic cleansing. The Apostle Paul in his first letter to the church at Thessalonica, wrote, "Now as to the times and the epochs, brethren, you have no need of anything to be written to you. For you yourselves know full well that the day of the Lord will come just like a thief in the night. While they are saying, 'Peace and safety!' then destruction will come upon them suddenly like birth pangs upon a woman with child; and they shall not escape." (1 Thessalonians 5:1-3) This will be the rational used to deceive the nations to assemble in the place called in Hebrew Armageddon. In their thinking, since the Jews are responsible for the lack of peace in the world, attributable to their faith in the God of the Bible, they will join in the movement to annihilate the Jews. These nations will not recognize this as Satan's strategy to retain his position as god of this world. At the same time this anti-Semitic feeling is causing the nations of the world to march to Israel to annihilate the Jews, the beast will be seeking out Christians to kill them. The beast will teach the same lies about Christians who refuse to worship the image of the beast. He will teach the world that their rebellion is causing globalization from occurring in the form that will bring peace. He will teach all the nations that all the suffering mentioned in

Revelation 16 is caused by Christians. He will further persuade the nations that the only way for The Bowls of Wrath to cease is to kill the Christians whose Lord is Jesus Christ, the King of Kings and Lord of Lords. (Revelation 16)

Questions:

1. Read Hebrews 9:27. What does this Scripture teach about reincarnation?

_____

_____

_____

2. Read about Jacob's trouble from Jeremiah 30:7-9. What events in those verses capture your attention and cause you to praise God?

_____

_____

_____

3. Do you think Babylon the Great is the great city, Jerusalem? Read Jeremiah 50-51 and Revelation 18.

_____

_____

_____

4. What are the goals of globalization that are fulfilled in the government led by the beast?

_____

_____

_____

5. Read John 8:44. What about Satan's character can be reflected in America today?

_____

_____

_____

6. Have you been challenged about your prayer life in his book? How?

_____

_____

_____

7. Does your church teach the importance of prayer? If not, what can you do to draw attention to it as part of the armor of God?

_____

_____

_____

8. What can you do to be the "salt and light" you as an individual are called to be as a Jesus follower?

_____

_____

_____

Chapter Fourteen

In 2 Thessalonians 2:3ff, the Apostle Paul wrote that the "spirit of lawlessness" had already gone out into the world. Before 100 A.D. lawlessness was already trying to find a foothold in the world's societies. The spirit of lawlessness is personified in by the Devil described in John 8:44 as a liar and murderer. This spirit of lawlessness continues to this day. Who hasn't been alarmed by the violence in the cities of America over these past months? In addition to this, the Apostle John wrote that the Spirit of Anti-Christ is already in the world. (1 John 4:3) That spirit is found in teachers who proclaim Jesus is not from God. They say there is nothing special about him. In contrast are those who "confess that Jesus Christ has come in the flesh." (1 John 4:2) The Apostle Paul wrote to Timothy, "I solemnly charge you in the presence of God and of Jesus Christ, who is to judge the living and the dead, and by his appearance and is kingdom, preach the word; be ready in season and out of season, reprove, rebuke, exhort, with great patience and instruction." (2 Timothy 4:1-2) To thwart what Satan is seeding into our various societies around the world, the church has to stand against it! (Ephesians 6:10-11) "Finally, be strong in the Lord and in the strength of his might. Put on the full armor of God that you may be able to stand firm against the schemes of the devil."

In the words of Jesus, it is the believers in Jesus Christ, who comprise his church, who are to do something about the condition of our country. Before we can do that, the church needs to light a fire in the lives of its members. Are you excited on a Sunday morning because you are going to be attending "church"? Are there great expectations about what God has for you to experience as you assemble with other believers in Jesus Christ? On the way, are you excited by the prospect of becoming "holy as God is holy" (1 Peter 1:16) Are you excited to learn more about what is being taught in the Bible, what God has said and how it applies to your life? Are you excited that God may have something to say to you? Are you looking forward to enlisting again in the army of God, namely the church, which is conducting spiritual warfare? Don't you want to hear how your fellow soldiers are doing as they fight alongside you as they share their testimonies about how your brothers and sisters in Christ are holding up in the battle? Are you excited as a soldier of the cross to be going to a training class to learn to fight with the weapons of our warfare? (2 Corinthians 10:4) According to that verse, they are powerful for the destruction of fortresses! Hopefully, you're not going to church to see what earrings so and so is wearing today. Indeed, the church is a beauty parlor as the Apostle Peter described it in 1 Peter 3:1-6, "In the same way, you wives, be submissive to your own husbands so that even if any of them are disobedient to the word, they may be won without a word by the behavior of their wives, as they observe your chaste and respectful behavior. And let not your adornment be external only--- braiding the hair, and wearing gold jewelry, and putting on dresses; but let it be the hidden person of the heart, with the imperishable quality of a gentle and quiet spirit, which is precious in the sight of God. For this is the way in former times the holy women also, who hoped in God, used to adorn themselves, being submissive to their own husbands." According to this verse, the church is to be a beauty parlor for women. The church is to have a way for the older women who have practiced these things to help the younger ones learn. The church does not exist as a fashion show where women model the latest fashions. The dress code for a worshipper is to reveal that the believer understands that "they are fearfully and wonderfully made." (Psalm 139) They are image bearers in need of grace. The Apostle Peter is saying that the church is a place to model fashion, but not for the outer man, but for the inner person of the heart. The styles that are popular are a gentle and quiet spirit. The Apostle Peter is not being Platonic when emphasizing the inner man, indeed we are to care for our bodies too. The Apostle Paul says we are to love and care for our bodies when talking about marriage. In Ephesians 5:25-29 wrote that husbands are to "love their wives as their own bodies... for no one ever hated his own flesh, but nourishes and cherishes it." Therefore, our wardrobes should reflect that we are "image bearers" and members of God's family.

Evangelical churches are not in competition with one another. They all have the same Biblical goal which is to present each member "mature in Christ" defined as "speaking the truth in love." (Ephesians 4:15) Ministers in each town can work together to inaugurate food kitchens, and good will stores to meet the physical needs of their community. They can sponsor evangelistic events like crusades. I remember as a young boy that the song leader for the Billy Graham crusades had a family who were members of our church. Together, our church worked with others to have Billy Graham come and speak at our town's football stadium. At a church I pastured in Indiana, we sponsored an evangelistic gathering where an illusionist working for Campus Crusade for Christ came, and amongst his many illusions, he inserted Gospel truths about our Lord Jesus Christ. Sharing a meal together can also be an important part of the fellowship the members of the church can enjoy together. Jesus alluded to this in Revelation 3:20 when he said, "Behold, I stand at the door and knock. If anyone hears my voice and opens the door, I will come into him and will <u>dine</u> with him, and he with me."

Sharing a meal together represented a bond that existed between those eating together. Not only does Jesus knock on the outer door of our heart and asks permission to enter our lives, forgive us our sins, and make us his children, he also knocks on individual doors in our lives and asks permission to enter. For example, he knocks on the door labeled husband. Once we allow him to enter, he works to make us a faithful and loving mate for our wife. He then knocks on the door labeled father. Once we open this area of our life to Jesus, he enters and makes us better fathers. He teaches us how not to provoke our children to anger, but rather "bring them up in the discipline and instruction of the Lord." (Ephesians 6:4) In his letter to the church at Thessalonica, Paul refers to how a father encourages and admonishes his children which he teaches us to do as fathers."(1 Thessalonians 2:9) Jesus then goes on to knock on all the other doors that reflect our activity like businessman and economist as we handle the finances of our home. The church at Corinth had not learned the importance of eating together as a sign of fellowship. Paul wrote to them and said, "For, in the first place, when you come together as a church, I hear that divisions exist among you...for in your eating each one takes his own supper first; and one is hungry, and another drunk." (1 Corinthians 11:20-21) I can remember almost 70 years ago our church having an outside picnic together. As a pastor, I loved the smorgasbords we enjoyed as a church family. I sensed the oneness we enjoyed together in that setting.

Even churches in the same community with the same Biblical goals seem isolated from one another. Sometimes there is contention. A church on one street corner sings "are there any stars in my crown?" while the church on the other side of the street sings, "No not one, no not one" and the church on the other corner sings "that will be glory, yes glory for me". One person has quipped, "to live above with saints aglow, that will be glory. However, to live below with saints we know, now that is another story."

That is a sad commentary on the condition of some churches. Jesus spoke to the church at Laodicea and said he wished her to be hot or cold, but not lukewarm. That is not how God wants the church to look to the casual observer. The church is the greatest wonder of the world. The book of Ephesians describes it as follows: Chapter One-"Made rich through the blessings of God;" Chapter Two-"Made alive through the love of God;" Chapter Three-"Made a dwelling by the mystery of God;" Chapter Four-"Made to walk by the Spirit of God;" Chapter Five-"Made into the likeness of Christ by the word of God;" and finally, Chapter Six-"Made to stand by means of the armor of God." In Ephesians 1:23 the Apostle Paul wrote that the church "is his body, the fullness of him who fills all in all." The church needs a make-over. We need to ask God, our beautician, to come and make the churches in America and around the world into his original design, the greatest wonder of the world.

There are some practical ways the church can function. Men's clubs in the church can be very helpful in giving men opportunities to do things together like golf, tennis, shuffle board, etc. After a certain age, men need men their own age with whom they can sit and laugh and do things together. When they have a pastor to direct their time together around spiritual truths and activities, so much the better. Many men are lonely and need friendship. The church can provide that environment where men can meet and pray together and study God's word. Younger men can meet together and learn the importance of serving. They can be directed to preparing and serving a meal to the women of the church. They can be directed to take a name out of hat and for a month, incognito do things for that individual. Couples can invite neighbors over to dinner. Couples together in the church can by tickets to a baseball game and take their neighbors with them to enjoy the game and later return to the church for a short time of refreshments together. The church can plan to have a booth at the local fair and give away a cup of cold water in the Lord's name to the thirsty passer bys. I suggested we do this at two churches where I was the pastor and it was well received by the church and the community. I am just throwing out a few ideas whereby the church can become active in the community. Other ways include sending a delegate to the school board meetings or city planning commission meetings. Be creative and active as a church. Start first with prayer whereby your church becomes the greatest wonder of your community.

Now as I close this book. Consider this! What would happen if Satan were successful in completely annihilating every Jew from the face of the earth? The Bible would be in error as to how the book of Revelation ended. Satan would remain god of this earth. There would be no Second Coming of the Lord Jesus Christ. There would be no thousand year rule of Christ. There would be no judgment at the end of the thousand year rule of Jesus Christ. The people in Hades would remain there forever. There would be no retribution for sins committed against people who were victims of crimes. The lawlessness in the world would increase to which there would be no end since the anti-Christ would continue to reign in Jerusalem. That means there would be hell on earth with people living constantly in fear. Rape, murder and crimes would be allowed since there would be no policing of our societies. There would be no more courts or judges handing down rulings. Justice would be a memory. The beast would be a perpetual government with no moral restraints. The voice of the church would be silenced since it would no longer exist. All Christians would be dead. No anti-government sentiment would be tolerated. The mark of the beast would be used to control all economic transactions. It would be used to monitor the whereabouts of all peoples on the earth. There would be no "freedom" for anyone. The public would be considered by the beast to be incapable of making "good" decisions for themselves. Therefore every action would need government approval before it could be done. The only worship done on earth would be that of Satan. There would no longer be a need to try camouflage his real entity as the one sitting in the holy of holies in the temple in Jerusalem. Though the Devil's existence would evidence four levels of life in God's creation, namely that of plant life, animal life, human beings and spirit beings, no one will be deducing truths like that. Plant life is species without spirit, animal life is soul in bondage to species, human beings are species in bondage to spirit and soul, while angels, whether good or bad, are spirit beings without species. People who deduce these truths in the last days will be killed if they voiced them. Satan, the father of lies, will dispel every truth about the true God. He will call it all "dis-information" as he has begun to do in our own society today. Every Bible and theology book would be burned as Satan would attempt to remove anything that would lead people to worship the true God.

There would be no funerals for deceased persons. During a person's life or in death there would be no mention of a person's afterlife. Because the Bible refers to one, there would be no Bibles or references to what the Bible said. Even though there would be nothing allowed that referenced God, that would not change the reality of what really happens to a person at death. The people alive on earth would sense that despite what they were taught about there being no afterlife, they would sense something different. This is because there is a sense of eternity written on their hearts. Part of the image of God retained in every individual after the Fall was rationality, morality and a sense of immortality. That is why Jesus taught that when the Holy Spirit would come, he would convict of sin, righteousness and judgment. In John 16:8-11 are recorded these words of our Lord Jesus Christ, "And he, when he comes, will convict the world of sin, righteousness and judgment; concerning sin, because they do not believe in me, concerning righteousness, because I go to the Father and you no longer behold me; and concerning judgment because the ruler of this world has been judged." Each part of the Image of God retained in mankind is addressed by the Holy Spirit. The Gospel has an appeal because that which is addressed by the Spirit of God has a corresponding receptivity because of the Image of God in them. Therefore the sense of immortality in mankind receives the idea of a future judgment. It is also the basis of understanding what happened at the crucifixion of the Lord Jesus Christ. A person's rationality accepts the premise that sin is a rebellion against God and when active it hurts others as the law of God is transgressed. The morality within man accepts the idea that something is owed to God as a result of sin. Also the person against whom sin is committed is owed retribution. That is why those killed during the tribulation period asked God for retribution for the sin against them. (Revelation 6:9-10) When a person sins, the guilt in their conscience screams for relief. When Jesus received what was due the sinner on the cross, what was due was paid for by the substitute God provided to pay for it. "All we like sheep have gone astray, we have turned everyone to his own way, but the Lord laid on him, the iniquity of us all." (Isaiah 53:6) When a sinner's sin and the guilt accompanying it are unpaid for, then like King David said after his sin with Bathsheba, "Wash me thoroughly from my iniquity, and cleanse me from my sin. For I know my transgressions, and my sin is ever before me...wash me and I shall be whiter than snow...Hide your face from my sins, and blot out all my iniquities. Create in me a clean heart, O God." (Psalm 51:2-10) Only God's forgiveness and restoration can create that clean spirit within us.

It is hard to imagine a society where there is no truth, a society that doesn't proclaim that after death we shall be assigned a place where we will spend eternity. Jesus told the story in Luke 16:19-31 of a rich man and a man named Lazarus. The insertion of the man's name keeps this story from being termed a parable. According to the story, each man died and went to Hades. Hades was divided into two parts divided by a wide gulf. On one side was Lazarus lounging in the luxury provided by Paradise. On the other side was a place of torment and agony called Hades. The rich man went there. Abraham and all the Old Testament saints who believed the promise given to them through Abraham were gathered there. All the people prior to Abraham who believed God's promise that a "he" born of a woman would come and destroy the effects of sin were also in Paradise, where Abraham was. When Jesus spoke to the thief on the cross, and promised him that he would take him to Paradise after he died, that is exactly where Jesus took him. He took him to Hades and specifically, that part of Hades called Paradise. In Ephesians 4:8-10 the Apostle Paul wrote that Jesus had once descended to the lower parts of the earth after his death. He further wrote that Jesus ascended with a host of captives and went to heaven. When the Apostle Paul wrote of his experience when he was taken into heaven, he mentioned that Paradise was now located there. Jesus took all the captives mentioned in Ephesians 4 where they were gathered in Paradise, back to heaven when he ascended. (2 Corinthians 12:4) The next time Hades in mentioned is in Revelation 20:11-15, "And I saw a great white throne and Him who sat upon it, from whose presence earth and heaven fled away, and no place was found for them. And I saw the dead, the great and the small, standing before the throne, and the books were opened, and another book was opened, which is the book of life, and the dead were judged from the things written in the books, according to their deeds. And the sea gave up the dead which were in it, and death and Hades gave up the dead which were in them; and they were judged, every one of them according to their deeds. And death and Hades were thrown into the Lake of fire. This is the second death, the lake of fire. And if anyone's name was not found written in the book of life, he was thrown into the lake of fire." Since there was no longer people alive on earth, there was no longer a need for a place for those who had ceased to live to go, namely death and Hades. Therefore they too were thrown into the lake of fire. This is what happens when Jesus returns to earth.

If all the Jews are killed, none of this happens. And how long there would be life on earth is unclear if Jesus doesn't return. What we know is that Jesus said "no life would have been saved" except for his return. (Matthew 24:22) There is much that is happening on this earth that is designed by the god of this world. He is plotting ways and establishing deceptive thinking which will ultimately provide him the basis for retaining that position. Consider 2 Corinthians 4:4 that the god of this world wants to retain that position and is constantly at work seeding the thoughts in all nations, including our own, that will yield fruit leading to his goal. Satan wants to retain the title of god on this earth. The purpose of this book is to expose the evil forces behind the current momentum towards a godless society. A Godless society would be the means Satan would use to implement his plan. The church as yet has not been taken from its position of restraining the Devil. (2 Thessalonians 2:6) Therefore, let's work, for Jesus said "Night would eventually fall when no more work can be done." (John 9:4) Our God is an awesome God. To live for him as he has designed and equipped us to live will make us "big-Godders." Therefore, let's rid ourselves of our small God mentality, and be the"Big-Godders" who will confront the Devil and the evil he attempts bring with him to America. Let all Jesus-followers become Big-Godders and unleash the power of God on America. The same power that raised Jesus from the dead (Philippians 3) is resident in all Jesus-followers so that we "cannot even ask or think of the things God is able to do through us." (Ephesians 3:20) So Let us begin asking our great God, who holds all that he created between his thumb and little finger, (Isaiah) to do great things as we, as "Big Godders," ask our God to do great things for his glory and honor. God said, "If my people who are called by my name will humble themselves and pray, and seek my face and turn from their wicked ways, then I will hear from heaven, will forgive their sin, and will heal their land." (2 Chronicles 7:14) Let's pray to that end.

Questions:

1. How many people do you think really understand to where their anti-Semitic rhetoric really leads?

_____

_____

_____

2. Describe your feelings after reading and studying the Scriptures in this book?

_____

_____

_____

3. What subject has impacted you most?

_____

_____

_____

4. What can you do to prepare your church to be the light and salt needed to make an impact on this world's thinking?

_____

_____

_____

5. What are your expectations on the way to your church?

_____

_____

_____

6. When you leave church, do you believe you have been equipped to battle the church's enemy?

_____

_____

_____

7. Do you now feel stronger and empowered in your prayer life? How is that going to change the way you pray?

_____

_____

_____

8. Recite the Lord's Prayer in your group or alone in your room. Give glory to God for his wonderful grace!

CPSIA information can be obtained
at www.ICGtesting.com
Printed in the USA
LVHW020326220222
711655LV00012BA/393